About

Choosing a College

Brandon Rogers

SPARK
COLLEGE

AN IMPRINT OF SPARK PUBLISHING

WWW.SPARKCOLLEGE.COM

Spark Publishing
120 Fifth Avenue
New York, NY 10011
www.sparknotes.com

ISBN 1-4114-0350-9

Please submit changes or report errors to **www.sparknotes.com/errors**

Printed and bound in Canada.

Library of Congress Cataloging-in-Publication Data available upon request.

CONTENTS

Why 10 Things?

It seems like everyone's writing books that claim to give you the basics, nice and simple—but what you get are pages overstuffed with lots of information you just don't need.

With *10 Things You Gotta Know*, we give you *exactly* what you need—no more, no less. We know you want your knowledge *now*, without wasting time on information that's not important. Learning 10 quick basics is the way to go.

Each 10 *Things* book contains:

- Lots of clear headings for skimming
- Sound bites of text that are easy to digest
- Sidebars that enhance your understanding
- Tons of Top 10 Lists for vital facts at a glance

Sure—maybe you could argue that there are 8 vital things, or 11. This isn't rocket science. But 10 is such a nice, even number—and who doesn't love a great Top 10?

In this book, we focus on 10 things you absolutely, positively gotta know about choosing a college:

1. **The Elite Schools**

   The crème de la crème, the cream of the crop, the dream schools of dream schools—we tell you what you need to know about the worshipped Ivy Leagues.

2. **The Public Ivies**

   Elite *public* schools? Everything you need to know, right here, right now, about getting a stellar education for a not-so-astronomical price.

3. **State Schools**

   A giant flagship university whose football team you may have rooted for throughout your childhood may be just the school for you.

4. **Liberal Arts Schools**

   Small classes, great professors, even—yes—ivy-covered walls . . . If you want to read deeply and think critically, one of these schools may be your perfect match.

5. **Fine Arts Schools**

   If you have a calling, a fine arts school may be the best place to hone your craft, meet like-minded peers, and kick-start your own body of work.

6. **Two-Year Schools**

   Whether you choose a community college or a technical school, one of these two-year options might give you exactly the education you want, at a price you can afford.

7. **Career Schools**

   You've seen their ads—but are they for you? We give you the lowdown on whether a for-profit career school makes sense for you.

8. **Distance-Learning Schools**

   Earn a degree without leaving your house—only a dream? Nope. Find out if this option fits your personality and learning style.

9. **Overseas Schools**

   It's time for college, and the world is your oyster. Don't rule these schools out just because they're far away from home.

10. **Treasure Schools**

    Not every student is a match for core classes and traditional activities—you may just find your niche at a school that defies easy categorization.

Before we get started, take a look at these 10 questions to see how much you really know about choosing a college. The answers follow.

1   You're perfect, and everyone loves you—you just *know* you want to go to Harvard. No second guessing, no second choices—the best school, the top school, is obviously the one for you, right?

    A. Obviously. You don't really know much about Harvard, but you just *know* you'll be happy there. You've always been drawn to brand names.

    B. You're in, end of story. Don't even bother sending an application. Harvard and the other Ivies hear about students like you and will knock on your door in approximately two weeks.

    C. College? Who has time to think about college? You have extracurriculars to attend to.

    D. It might be right for you—but investigate first, and don't assume you'll get in. You need to send a thoughtful, thorough application—*and* get a second choice.

2   You're a top-notch student, and you plan to attend the best college possible. You'll apply to a few Ivies, but you've heard that there are actually *public* universities out there where you could get a great education too. Could these schools be for you?

    A. No. You want to go to a *good* school, and everyone knows the Ivies are the best. You won't settle for a public school, no way.

    B. Public schools are for students without the brains you have. You're insulted to even consider it. You just wrote a paper on Nabokov for your English class, for pity's sake. You're a *smartie*.

    C. The world, darling, the entire *world* is below you. Public schools: no and no.

    D. You may have found your choice. Many of these public schools are just as good as the Ivy League schools—and can come at much more reasonable prices if you go to school in your home state.

3   Go UT! Go UT! Support for your state school has been bred into you
    since childhood. You always thought you'd go to the school that match-
    es the old blanket in the rec room—and the pennants on the wall of
    the garage—but your top priority for college is close interaction with
    full professors. Is a big state school right for you?

   A. Sure it is. It's a college, right? With classes? Faculty members will be
       everywhere.
   B. Football alone makes it right for you. Get your priorities in order: football
       then faculty.
   C. You *think* faculty is important, but you'll change your mind once you get
       swept up in the energy of Homecoming Weekend. As long as someone
       tells you what chapter to read, you'll get a fine education.
   D. Better check out other options. State schools are notorious for having
       teaching assistants teach their undergraduates.

4   For you, the ideal test is multiple-choice, and your favorite method of
    studying is to memorize long lists of facts, statistics, and information.
    Is a liberal arts college right for you?

   A. Sure it is. You'll ace your exams by memorizing all the handouts, just like
       you do now. So what if 70 percent of your grade is class participation?
       You'll fake it.
   B. You like to memorize, but you like not studying even more. You've heard
       that liberal arts schools don't even have exams. Awesome.
   C. Forget college. You're going to become famous for memorizing ten thou-
       sand digits of *pi*. Maybe more.
   D. If you can adapt your study method, this choice might be right for you.
       But since liberal arts schools emphasize a different style of learning, you
       may find that it's not the best match for your abilities.

5   You spend your days and nights dreaming of painting your way into the Guggenheim. Your bedroom is overrun with canvasses and art supplies. The thought of spending the next four years on anything other than your art gives you panic attacks. Is college out of the question?

   A. You're an artist, not a student. School for the likes of you would be a complete waste of time and money.

   B. College? You'll take the school of life, thanks. That's the only way you'll truly become an *Artist* with a capital A.

   C. Your parents are footing the college bill, so it's not like you have to *study*. You'll just skip class and paint in your dorm room. Wanted: a roommate who doesn't mind the smell of paint thinner.

   D. College could be just what you need to take your art to the next level. There are schools out there designed for artists-in-training, just like you.

6   There's one main thing that matters to you when it comes to your college education: you want to maximize your chances of getting a job immediately after graduating. In fact, you want your education to consist of practical, real-life training in a particular field, and you'd like to do it in about two years. What kind of college is right for you?

   A. The school of life. Get in there, roll your sleeves up, and turn burger-flipping into an art form.

   B. What college *isn't* right? is the question. You care about a job, not classes. You'll be counting down the minutes till four years of Renaissance lit and philosophy are over.

   C. Definitely a distance-learning school. Then you can get a degree and work wherever you want without missing a beat.

   D. A two-year technical school will be your best bet. These are generally vocation-focused and will give you lots of real-world work experience that will help you kick-start your career.

7   You're a nontraditional student with a family, and you want to change careers. You want to become licensed as a cosmetologist and eventually open your own salon. What school is right for you?

   A. A liberal arts school, where you can take an art history class and learn about beauty through the ages. None of it will help you get your cosmetology license, but your work will be *informed*.

B. An elite school with lots of tuition-poor students who will let you practice on them for a cool $5.

C. A distance-learning school, so no one can see the mistakes you make when you attempt a radical makeover on yourself.

D. A career school that will give you hands-on experience in your field, which will help you get licensed in your field of choice.

8   **You live in a small, rural town that isn't within driving distance of your state university, and you want to earn your bachelor's degree. Short of relocating, do you have any options?**

A. You can homeschool yourself, just for the fun of it. You won't end up with a degree, but you can amuse your neighbors with fun facts from the psych textbook you bought online.

B. Why *not* relocate? This is your education we're talking about. Family, jobs, and other commitments will just have to step aside.

C. Do one of those "PH.D. IN 10 DAYS" programs you read about in the emails that always clutter up your email account. Sounds like the perfect fit.

D. Enroll in a distance-learning school. You can work from home, make your own schedule, and, if you choose the right school, earn a respectable degree.

9   **The world is out there, and you're ready to see it—*now*. But when you tell people you want to go to college in Paris, they just laugh and tell you to go watch *Amélie*. Is your idea really that crazy?**

A. Yes, it is. Your parents driving you to college in their station wagon is the whole point of college.

B. It's not crazy, but it's too far, too different, and too adventurous. Doing what everyone else is doing has always served you well; why stop now?

C. You could barely afford your high school band uniform—a foreign college is way, way out of the realm of possibility. Dream on.

D. Your idea is excellent, not crazy. Going to college abroad might be the life-changing experience you're looking for.

10 You've always enjoyed hearing your cousins' stories about college, and you've even flipped through some of their textbooks and accompanied them to class. And you know one thing for sure: you don't want it for yourself. You want to go to college, but you need something different. Will you ever find a school that's right for you?

A. Whoa, picky. You're different, you're unique, yadda yadda yadda. Choose a school already. It's not rocket science.

B. You're obviously hoping for something no student in the world has ever wished for, ever before, so just give up now. There's no hope for you. Next.

C. Will you ever find a school? Sure. There are hundreds of colleges out there. Since nothing will make you happy, just draw a name from a hat. It may not be the right school, but it will be something.

D. Of course you'll find a school, but you need to look beyond the standard categories. There are many excellent colleges out there that are tailored to students who are looking for something a little different.

Answers

1

Answer: D. Elite schools like Harvard accept a very small percentage of applicants every year, and even with your stellar academic record, there's no guarantee you'll have the *je ne sais quoi* that will get you in the door. And just because the Ivies are great schools doesn't mean they're the right ones for you—so do your research. **See Chapter 1.**

2

Answer: D. Some public universities are so good that they're called the Public Ivies—so don't cross a school off your list because it's not called Yale or Princeton. One of these schools may actually be an even better choice for you. **See Chapter 2.**

3

Answer: D. State universities are generally more focused on graduate studies and faculty research than on undergraduate teaching, which means graduate student teaching assistants may teach many of your classes, at least for the first couple of years. If you want small classes taught by full professors, a smaller school is probably a better option for you. **See Chapter 3.**

4

Answer: D. Liberal arts schools require students to do more than just memorize material. You'll learn how to read carefully, think critically, and write well about all kinds of subjects. **See Chapter 4.**

5

Answer: D. Fine arts schools can be a great option if you're driven to develop your art, whether it be painting, poetry, performance, or anything else. You'll get an education that will allow you to learn and do art, and you'll be swaddled in a community of like-minded students. **See Chapter 5.**

6

Answer: D. Technical schools focus more on job skills training than academics per se. So if you know you want to start a career in automotive repair, for example, you'll receive specific training to help you reach your goal. **See Chapter 6.**

7

Answer: D. Career schools are targeted at individuals who want to get job skills training in a particular field. These schools are for-profit, and you should investigate the quality carefully, but they can be a great choice if you need a stepping stone to get you started in your chosen career. **See Chapter 7.**

8
Answer: D. As distance learning increases in popularity, more and more universities are offering distance-learning options. Online colleges, too, can give you a quality education. Distance learning isn't for everyone, but it might be the right option for you. **See Chapter 8.**

9
Answer: D. You may arrive on campus with a suitcase instead of a station wagon, but going to college abroad might be exactly right for you. And good news: you can even get federal financial aid to help you pay for it. **See Chapter 9.**

10
Answer: D. Not every college is an elite school, or a state school, or any other easily labeled type. We call these "treasure schools" because sometimes they take a little work to find—and because they're worth the search. One of these schools might be the perfect fit for you.
See Chapter 10.

INTRODUCTION

"I am not an adventurer by choice but by fate."

Vincent van Gogh

It's time to choose a college—overwhelmed yet? Don't panic. There's a lot of information out there, so your goal is to become as empowered as you possibly can be. Learning the basics about the types of schools available is the first step in making an informed, excellent choice—and that's exactly what we give you in *10 Things You Gotta Know About Choosing a College*. But before you begin reading about schools, you need to know about the other nitty-gritties: college admissions, college rankings, and financial aid.

10 Admissions Basics

There's a lot of information out there about college admissions, and understanding the terminology will keep you from feeling confused and help you make better decisions about what college is right for you. There are (you guessed it) 10 important new terms and phrases you should know.

1. Enrollment Management

Colleges rely on students to keep their motors running, and so they operate like a business. Like any good business, colleges have to do more than just attract customers: they have to build a product image. Colleges refer to the process by which they attract, retain, and graduate students as *enrollment management*.

Long gone are the days when just a handful of elite colleges existed to educate a very small portion of the population. College has rapidly become a near universal expectation, which means a lot of colleges have popped up over the last century, and most will be in fierce competition with each other to stay afloat. The seller's mantra of "the customer is always right" should come in quite handy as you shop for a school—remember, *you're* going to improve the *college*, not just vice versa.

2. The Admissions Officer

The admissions officer is definitely someone you should get to know—he or she will be your point person for information and support when you're applying to a school. The category of "admissions officer" includes several different types of people:

- Admissions counselors

- Assistant directors of admissions
- Directors of admissions
- Deans

Admissions officers are concerned with finding great students and getting them to enroll in the schools they represent.

3. The Gatekeeper

Almost every admissions officer has two basic personalities: the gatekeeper and the salesman. Admissions officers want to make sure that the student body is as strong as possible, and this personality is known among the admissions profession as the "gatekeeper." Gatekeepers won't let just anybody in—they want only those students who represent the best fit for the college.

4. The Salesman

Only a tiny percentage of colleges have the luxury of turning away 70 percent or more of their applicants, so admissions officers have to serve as "salesmen" as well. The salesman wants to sell the college, which often means that you'll hear a lot about what makes the college so special and very little about what could be improved.

The gatekeeper and the salesman are often in conflict. As a prospective student, your goal should be to draw out the gatekeeper side, not only to find out if you are truly what the college is looking for, but also to find out if this college is right for you.

5. The Rep

Admissions officers aren't the only people willing to sing the praises of a specific college. Colleges will often use a wide variety of individuals to get the word out about their schools, and these people can be an even greater resource

"Everything I heard from the admissions counselor about the college just seemed too good to be true. But then I talked with someone who actually went to the college. He gave me the whole story, which also included some criticism of campus life. I appreciated his honesty, and still wound up enrolling."

Heather
University of Virginia

for you in your quest to find the perfect match. Admissions representatives, or "reps," can include students, alumni, professors, and other college staff. These representatives may not be able to answer very specific questions about a college—such as the teacher/student ratio—but they can be a great source of insider information and are probably more likely to give you the *real* story about a college, rather than a rosy sales pitch.

6. The Funnel

The admissions funnel refers to the stages of the admissions process, from student inquiries all the way to student enrollees. College staff call it a "funnel" because there are typically a lot more inquiries at the top, which gradually narrow down to a relatively small number of students who actually apply. An admissions counselor's first goal is to generate a large number of student inquiries and turn as many of those inquiries as possible into actual applicants.

Colleges will classify you as an inquiry as soon as you approach them with a question, such as by filling out an information card. Afterward, they'll probably add you to their mailing list and, in some cases, a phone list. Unless you have already decided specifically which college you want to attend, there's nothing wrong with being at the top of the funnel for whatever colleges interest you. Be prepared to receive plenty of colorful catalogs and the occasional phone call asking if you're still interested in a particular school.

7. The Review

An admissions review is the process that colleges use to determine who gets an offer of admission. This process often involves a numerical formula that weighs a student's attributes, including things like GPA, test scores, extracurricular activities, essays, and interviews. Although they

From Inq to App

Admissions officers are often evaluated by how many inquiries ("inqs") they can turn into applicants ("apps"). Colleges that are struggling to meet their enrollment goals will even have incentives to get students to apply, such as waiving the application fee or offering tuition awards. As you speak with college representatives, be sure and ask for any benefits you can get.

may not ever reveal how you scored, you should still ask to see the formula they use, which will often give you a very good idea of your chances for admission. Knowing this formula may also help you decide which safety schools to consider.

8. The Safety School

A safety school is a college where you have a high likelihood of gaining admission. Once you've narrowed down the schools you'll apply to, you should include at least two or three safety schools. Don't let the name fool you—some safety schools are real gems.

9. The Open House

Colleges have several ways of introducing themselves to prospective students, one of which is known as an *open house*. Open houses, as the name implies, refer to specific dates that colleges set aside for campus visits. On these occasions, a college puts its best foot forward, sometimes even allowing visitors to sit in on classes. A great thing about an open house is that it will allow you to gain as much information about a specific college in as short a time as possible. Colleges typically announce open houses on their websites and through local television channels, radio stations, and newspapers.

10. The College Fair

Few students have the time or money to visit every open house. Fortunately, many colleges participate in regional or national college fairs. Prospective students can get the most bang for their buck at these events, which sometimes have information booths representing hundreds of schools. The largest college fair organizer is the National Association for College Admission Counseling (NACAC). Visit www.nacac.com to find out when a college fair may be coming to your area and which schools will be participating.

The Rankings

You've no doubt heard about college rankings, which essentially crown the king and queen of higher education. But don't make the mistake of allowing

10

Statistics That Matter

1
Average class size

2
Student-to-faculty ratio

3
Percentage of students who graduate

4
Matriculation rate

5
Percentage of applicants who gain admission

6
Number of applicants

7
Average test scores

8
Average GPA

9
Percentage of students who receive loans

10
Percentage of students who receive grants or scholarships

your college choice to come down to an opinion in a magazine you never even read. Rankings provide great publicity for the few colleges selected as the "best," but in the end, the only judgment that matters is your own. You wouldn't let a group of reporters choose your next boyfriend or girlfriend—and letting them choose your next college might not be such a wise move either.

Rankings Dangers

One danger in relying too heavily on rankings is that you might come away with the idea that only two or three hundred colleges exist in the United States. In truth, if you consider each school eligible for federal financial aid in the United States, you have over 6,000 choices, only a relatively small percentage of which ever receive much attention. Less than 10 percent of all colleges receive any major press coverage in the ratings game, and the odds should tell you that the college that's right for you could be one that many people have never heard of.

Also problematic is that sometimes the best schools fall through the cracks. Many of the nationally recognized ranking systems do not actually rank every college. In fact, one of the most academically rigorous schools in the country, Reed College in Portland, Oregon, never even fills out the *U.S. News and World Report* surveys. In short, the rankings are a great indication of *what other people like*, and since there's a good chance that you are you and not some other person, your best bet is to rely on your own judgment in picking the right school.

How Rankings Can Help

This is not to say that college rankings have no purpose. As long as you understand the formula being used, rankings can be useful. Some common criteria often used by college ratings guides include average class size, percentage of applicants who gain admission, and the average test scores and grade point averages of incoming students. Most rating systems can also tell you a little bit about costs and the percentage of students who receive financial aid.

Of course, in some aspects, many small public colleges have virtually the same statistics as the Ivy League schools, with sometimes smaller class sizes,

You can also get this same information from many guides and websites, including **www. sparkcollege.com**.

lower student-to-faculty ratios, and even higher graduation rates. So why do the same few elite colleges consistently find themselves atop the ratings charts? Selectivity and reputation are two factors that play an important role in how colleges rank. One of these top-rated schools might indeed be the ideal college for you—just don't base your decision entirely on a top-ten list.

The Cost

College finances will probably play a role in which college turns out to be your ideal match. Since the most expensive colleges could set you back over $100,000 for a bachelor's degree, and with tuition rising between 5 and 10 percent every year, the influence of the price tag will grow only stronger as time goes by. More and more students have to ask themselves just how much they're willing to pay for tuition before the right educational choice becomes the wrong financial decision.

Your Worth

Many colleges use famous student alumni to help define their image.

Only you and your parents can determine the formula for what your bottom line is financially. Some students who think they'll eventually land a high-paying career might determine that $60,000 worth of student loan debt is reasonable. However, a high college price tag does not automatically convert into a high-paying career. Remember, with the perfect college, you are entering into a mutually beneficial relationship requiring a combined effort. Yes, the right college will make you better, but your skills and talent will also help make the college a better place.

A good attitude with which to approach choosing a college is to seriously consider any college that seriously considers you. This means looking twice at colleges that recognize the contribution you have to make by offering you significant financial aid. Many students take an "at any cost" attitude when it comes to their dream college. However, no matter how prestigious the school, if it is charging you full tuition, then you really have to consider whether your relationship is getting off to the best start.

Your Money Plan

No matter where you are in the college search process, you need to formulate a financial aid plan of attack, which means more than completing all the required financial aid forms on time. When you start visiting colleges, you should always include a visit to the financial aid office. Each college has its own unique financial aid forms and deadlines, and it's vital that you get that information.

In addition, don't be afraid to take a creative approach toward funding your higher education. For example, as graduate degrees become more and more popular, many clever students have figured out that earning a four-year undergraduate degree at an affordable state college and pursuing a two-year graduate degree at a prestigious private college makes more sense financially. Also, for years students have earned associate's degrees at community and technical colleges before transferring to a four-year college to earn their bachelor's degrees, saving thousands of dollars in the process.

The Good News

The college financial aid picture does have some bright spots. In fact, many of the most expensive colleges have recently announced sweeping reforms to what they charge students with financial need. Yale, for example, no longer expects students whose families earn less than $45,000 per year to pay for their education, and families earning between $45,000 and $60,000 per year will have their expected contributions reduced as well. No matter how intimidating a college's sticker price may seem on the outside, never automatically write off your chances.

About This Book

To give you the clearest picture possible of the types of schools available to you, we've divided each chapter into—surprise!—10 sections. These are the 10 basic things you need to know to decide which kind of college is right for you. They'll help you determine where you can get in, where you'll fit in, and, most important, where you'll be most happy. The big 10 are:

1. Selectivity
2. Reputation
3. Cost
4. Academics
5. Campus life
6. Residential life
7. Atmosphere
8. Students
9. Professors
10. The Intangibles

Each chapter begins with a list of 10 clues that the school might not be right for you—so you can decide right away whether you should even turn the page.

As you look through the next 10 chapters, be prepared to keep an open mind: you might find that your choices are much different from what you've always thought. And remember: you're not just looking for the best college—you're looking for the right college for *you*.

1

THE ELITE SCHOOLS

"Why was Penn the right choice? I needed a school that believes in the high expectations I set for myself. When it came down to picking a college, I wanted nothing less than the best education in the world."

Kate
University of Pennsylvania

10 CLUES

They Might *Not* Be for You

1

You're not driven by near perfection when it comes to grades or test scores.

2

You rank *competitiveness* somewhere near the top of your pet peeves.

3

You're looking for a place where you can be a big fish in a small pond.

4

The thought of interviewing for college admissions drives you to your "happy place."

5

You can't see yourself under any circumstances writing an essay as a condition of applying to a college.

6

You're looking for a college where you can quietly blend in with the crowd.

7

You're hoping to pay off your student loans sometime in the next century.

8

You don't want to move very far away for college. And you live in Alaska.

9

You suffer from sesquipedalophobia (a fear of long words).

10

Word association: someone says "ivy," you say "poison."

The Ivy League refers to eight schools that formed an agreement in 1945 to regulate their football competitions:

- **Brown**
- **Columbia**
- **Cornell**
- **Dartmouth**
- **Harvard**
- **University of Pennsylvania**
- **Princeton**
- **Yale**

Today, most people know the Ivy League schools for their prowess inside the classroom, not on the football field. Harvard, Yale, and Princeton, in particular, have become associated in popular culture with the pinnacle of academic superiority. Add to the stellar reputation of these colleges a list of alumni who have become leaders in the worlds of business, politics, and the arts, and the result is an unequaled level of selectivity and prestige.

The great thing about higher education in the United States is that if you dream big, work hard, and have a personality that shines through, you may be just the right student for one of these elite schools. However, the most important question is whether an elite college is right for *you*.

At a Glance

Though every school is different, all schools in the "elite" category share some common traits. You probably have an image in your mind of what these schools are like, but understanding the following 10 nitty-gritty basics is the only way to tell if one of them is your perfect match.

1. Selectivity

You may be certain that an Ivy League college is right for you, but the feeling might not be mutual. The percentage of applicants admitted to these schools ranges from 10 percent at ultraselective Harvard and Yale to the nearly 30 percent acceptance rate at Cornell, the Ivy League school with the largest student body.

As the saying goes, though, the hardest thing about the Ivy League is getting in. For the most part, eventual Ivy League students have been planning for years on acquiring the grades, test scores, academic and extracurricular achievements, and nerves of steel needed for admission. In fact, one of the unique challenges of deciding if an Ivy League school is right for you is deciding if the *process* of applying to an Ivy League school is right for you.

Graduating in the top 5 percent of your high school class and getting a perfect score on your SAT just aren't enough for many of these institutions—it's often said that the Ivy League schools could admit *only* students with perfect SATs and still have no trouble filling their first-year class. Despite your many accomplishments, you still may need a little luck. Even if you have a stellar academic record, you'll probably want to consider applying to a few colleges with less selective admissions as part of your backup plan.

2. Reputation

Admit it: whether it's the best car, the best clothes, or the best college, designer labels have a powerful attraction. "Ivy League" has a particularly nice ring to it. Without question, having an Ivy League school on your résumé will cause future employers and grad schools to look twice, and your friends and family will feel rightly proud of you. That reputation breeds success on campus as well, with Ivy League schools consistently drawing not only the best and the brightest students, but also teachers, artists, world leaders, and other VIPs, many of whom attended these very schools themselves.

Don't let the reputation mislead you, however. Depending on what you want to study, the Ivy League schools may not, in fact, be your best choice. This holds particularly true for engineering, computer science, and other highly technical programs. Additionally, if your dream job is in a relatively lower paying profession, such as social work or nonprofit administration, the stellar reputation may come at too high a tuition cost.

3. Cost

A world-class education doesn't come cheap. Ivy League schools have long held the distinction of being among the priciest colleges in the country, with tuition currently averaging around $27,000 per year. But cost alone shouldn't keep you from considering whether one of these colleges is right for you. The Ivy League schools, unlike many other private colleges, have enough resources to meet your financial need through scholarships. A few examples:

- Dartmouth's average scholarship exceeds $24,000.
- Brown will meet the demonstrated financial need of any admitted student.
- In February 2004, Harvard announced that students from households earning less than $40,000 will not have any tuition or room/board payments.
- Yale will not require anyone with a family income below $45,000 to pay any portion of his or her education.

Many students, in fact, have discovered that the Ivy League colleges can be a great financial bargain. With the Ivy League schools, you don't always get what you pay for. Sometimes you get a whole lot more.

4. Academics

Remember, the Ivy League schools attract the brightest students in the world. Academic life goes on both inside and outside the classroom, and graduates will consistently tell you they learned as much from discussions with their

One of the Ivy League colleges, Cornell, is also New York State's public land grant college. New York State residents who apply to Cornell's schools of Agriculture, Human Ecology, and Industrial/Labor Relations pay $17,200 per year in tuition, as opposed to the $31,300 charged to applicants at Cornell's other schools.

fellow students as they did from their textbooks. Although you may run into the occasional lecture hall with fifty to one hundred students, the typical experience in an Ivy League classroom involves small class discussions led by committed and caring faculty.

The difficulty of the coursework depends greatly on which school you attend and the major you select. In any case, the Ivy League schools generally graduate a high percentage of their students. Dartmouth, for example, retains 96 percent of its students and has a 92 percent graduation rate.

The students who have what it takes to gain admission here have what it takes to succeed anywhere. In other words, although you won't be *guaranteed* a degree, a fear of an impossibly hard curriculum shouldn't keep you from applying.

5. Campus Life

Cornell has the second largest Greek system in the nation.

When choosing the right college, remember that you'll spend far more time outside the classroom than inside it. You may wind up judging your overall experience by the quality of your extracurricular life, including the friends you make and your out-of-classroom activities. Here again, the Ivy League schools have a lot to offer, with some of the nation's oldest and most famous student groups.

Where else but at Harvard's Hasty Pudding can you ham it up at the nation's oldest undergraduate theatrical group? Where else but at Columbia can you express your sheer *joie de vivre* at the nation's oldest glee club? Where else but at Yale can you write for the nation's oldest college daily newspaper? Student groups at the Ivy League schools aren't just fun; they're world renowned, and participation in these extracurricular activities alone has launched careers.

10 Famous Clubs

1. Harvard: the Hasty Pudding theatrical group
2. Harvard: the *Harvard Lampoon*
3. Columbia: Glee Club
4. Penn: Philomathean Society (oldest literary society in the United States)
5. Princeton: Cottage Club
6. Yale: Skull and Bones
7. Dartmouth: The Outing Club
8. Dartmouth: *The Dartmouth*—the nation's oldest college newspaper
9. Brown University: Pacifica House
10. Cornell: Quill and Dagger, an honor society

In spite of the relatively small campus sizes, the Ivy League colleges offer plenty of choices. Dartmouth College, with a total student body of just 4,000, still offers more than 200 student groups. Cornell has over 600 student organizations. Greek life is alive and well at the Ivy League schools, so if you're intent on pledging with a fraternity or sorority, don't cross these colleges off your list.

6. Residential Life

Choosing the right Ivy League college may come down to what kind of campus housing you prefer. The Ivy League schools pride themselves on establishing a strong sense of community, which often begins in the residence halls. Housing options range from highly structured residential life systems to basic dormitories. Though students from private boarding high schools may be used to campus living, it can be a shock to the average public high school student—make sure you find out everything you can about your school of choice.

"The Residential College at Yale forced me to interact with people I might never have otherwise. It wound up being one of the best parts of my education."

Kevin
Yale University

 ESSENTIALS
To Get You in the Door

1

Sky-high GPA

2

Graduating in top 5 percent of your high school class

3

Stellar test scores

4

Superior writing skills

5

A solid record of extracurricular achievement

6

A world-class talent in music, athletics, or art

7

Proven leadership and motivation

8

The ability to ace a live interview

9

Glowing letters of recommendation

10

A fair helping of good luck

At one end of the spectrum sits the Residential College System at Yale, which may remind you a little of Harry Potter. Yale assigns all of its undergrads to one of twelve residential colleges, each with its own dean and master. These masters oversee the aspects of your educational and social programs. Each residential college also has its own library, dining hall, and tutors. Because Yale assigns you to your college, this means you'll interact with a diverse range of students whom you might not otherwise meet. While most alumni praise this arrangement, it might not be for you.

Though not as highly structured, the other Ivy League schools also emphasize the importance of living on campus to varying degrees. Nearly all Princeton and Harvard undergraduates live on campus, while at Cornell and Penn, just over half do so. Remember, if you're admitted, you need to act fast to arrange student housing. The best college housing is sometimes assigned on a first come, first served basis.

7. Atmosphere

These eight schools may fall under the same athletic division, but don't be fooled into thinking that if you visit one, you've visited them all. From tiny Dartmouth in rural New Hampshire to Columbia in New York City, the Ivy League campuses are probably more diverse than you think. Want a large campus? Cornell enrolls nearly 14,000 students. Looking for an urban setting? Harvard, Columbia, and Penn are based in Boston, New York City, and Philadelphia, respectively. If you prefer a more isolated locale, Dartmouth, Princeton, and Cornell, located in Hanover, New Hampshire; Princeton, New Jersey; and Ithaca, New York, might be good options.

Diversity on campus is important, and the Ivy League schools excel here, led by Penn's 41 percent minority enrollment.

You should also consider climate: all of the Ivy League colleges are located in the Northeast. Thinking about weather might seem strange or irrelevant, but weather is often the biggest source of complaints from students at many of these campuses. Dartmouth and Cornell, in particular, can have particularly harsh winters.

8. Students

You might think that the student bodies at these schools look more like Mensa reunions than groups of regular people. True, the elite colleges have far more applicants than slots, so they can pretty much make their campuses look any way they choose. Fortunately, they understand the importance of a diverse student body, and the students at the elite colleges come from all walks of life. Your classmates will come from upper, middle, and lower economic classes and from all cultures, races, and nationalities. What these students will generally have in common are superior academic records, a drive to be the absolute best, and the confidence that big things are headed their way.

9. Professors

Think it's hard to get into the Ivy League as a student? Don't expect much sympathy from the professors, who count themselves among the brightest and most talented people in the world. Want to learn writing from Nobel Prize–winning author Toni Morrison or physics from MacArthur Genius Award winner Paul Ginsparg? Then an Ivy League college could be the right choice for you.

Only a small handful of individuals have what it takes to teach at the very best colleges, and no matter what class you take, you'll find yourself in the presence of greatness. The Ivy League professors are known all over for their expertise and research. And though many earn nearly $200,000 per year, they often make much more through book sales, speaking engagements, and consultancy fees. Ivy League teachers are the rock stars of higher education.

Their celebrity can be intimidating at times. Although the Ivy League schools typically avoid teaching assistants, that doesn't mean that you're going to be guaranteed face time with superstars like Cornel West or Henry Louis Gates. And you know that saying, "The hardest thing about the Ivy League is getting into the Ivy League"? It's rooted in the claims made by some elite colleges that over half of its students receive A's in their classes. Apparently, some professors spend too much time on the speaking circuit and not enough time in the classroom, doing the kind of critical grading and evaluating that might cut down the number of A-level students. Keep in mind, though, that spending even a little time with the greatest minds in the world might not be such a bad trade-off when choosing a college with an Ivy League pedigree.

10. The Intangibles

The elite schools offer more than just a stellar education. If you value giving back to the community, you should ask college representatives about volunteer opportunities. The Ivy League schools have long been leaders in this arena. At Yale, over 75 percent of students actively participate in community service. The founders of many of the nation's major community service programs—from City Year to the Campus Outreach Opportunity League—graduated from Ivy League schools.

Harvard admits only around 50 out of every 1,000 transfer applicants each year, or around 5 percent.

Other factors to consider include study-abroad options. For many Ivy Leaguers, their education would be incomplete without a trip overseas. At Dartmouth, over 60 percent of students spend at least a quarter abroad, and over 1,200 students at Penn studied at 36 foreign countries in 2002.

10

FAMOUS
Ivy League Alums

1

Penn: Ezra Pound

2

Cornell: Kurt Vonnegut

3

Cornell: Janet Reno

4

Brown: John F. Kennedy, Jr.

5

Dartmouth: Theodore Seuss Geisel (Dr. Seuss)

6

Harvard: Theodore Roosevelt

7

Princeton: F. Scott Fitzgerald

8

Columbia: Langston Hughes

9

Columbia: Alicia Keys

10

Yale: Jodie Foster

If you've thought about taking some time off between high school and college, you're in luck: the elite colleges recognize the value of taking a break. Harvard encourages students to defer enrollment for up to one year, as long as they don't enroll at another college. You might decide to travel, pursue a special project, or enroll in a service program such as AmeriCorps.

With such an overwhelming number of students wanting to get into the elite schools, second chances at the Ivy Leagues are few and far between. If you're offered admission, you'll need to decide quickly if this is the right choice for you. The common strategy of attending a cheaper two-year college and transferring for your final two years of school generally won't work at the Ivy League colleges.

The Other Elites

A diverse range of colleges can be even more selective than the Ivy Leagues. They represent a small sample of the other elites, schools that are extremely competitive, offer outstanding academic programs, and attract the best and brightest students and faculty.

Many of these elite colleges, such as Stanford and Duke, are well known. But you may never have heard of some of the others, such as:

- Davidson College in Davidson, North Carolina
- Macalester College in St. Paul, Minnesota
- Washington University in St. Louis, Missouri

Typically, but not always, these colleges are similar in atmosphere to the Ivy League colleges. They often have relatively small enrollments, diverse but competitive student bodies, and rigorous course loads. They can also charge a small fortune, with many even more expensive than the Ivy League schools.

FAMOUS
Ivy League Professors

1

Toni Morrison, author: Princeton

2

Paul Ginsparg, MacArthur Genius Award winner: Cornell

3

Peter Singer, humanitarian: Princeton

4

Henry Louis Gates, Jr., African American Studies scholar: Harvard

5

Joyce Carol Oates, author: Princeton

6

Dr. Lawrence Klein, Nobel Prize winner in economics: Penn

7

Jane Goodall, professor-at-large: Cornell

8

Carlos Fuentes, professor-at-large: Brown

9

John Rassias, foreign language professor: Dartmouth

10

Horst Stormer, Nobel Prize–winner in physics: Columbia

10 Other Elites

There are many more than 10 schools that qualify as "the other elites." This list represents just a sampling.

1. The Massachusetts Institute of Technology
2. The Juilliard School (New York)
3. The United States Military Academy (New York)
4. Stanford University (California)
5. Notre Dame University (Indiana)
6. Duke University (North Carolina)
7. Vanderbilt University (Tennessee)
8. Bowdoin College (Maine)
9. George Washington University (Washington, DC)
10. Wesleyan University (Connecticut)

Ten MIT faculty members have won the Nobel Prize, and Stanford counts fourteen Nobel Laureates among its faculty while the California Institute of Technology has four.

Is This the Right Choice?

The elite colleges have no shortage of students eager to enter through their shiny gates, and with admission rates between only 10 and 20 percent, the question of whether an Ivy League school is right for you may very well be out of your hands. However, these schools offer some compelling advantages that may convince you to apply. First, the elite colleges can afford to hire the best and brightest professors and purchase the latest equipment and facilities. Add small class sizes and meaningful student-faculty interaction to the formula and you have a recipe for academic success.

The elite colleges also have a canny ability to attract not only the absolute best faculty but also the best students and staff. Those who have excelled in their fields naturally want to surround themselves with other accomplished individuals. The elite colleges also do an admirable job of creating extremely diverse student bodies, so don't worry that an "old boy's network" will hurt your chances of admission.

Most of the elite colleges have tuition rates to match their level of esteem, but don't let this keep you from applying. These colleges also often have large endowments, and many will meet your entire level of financial need, keeping your costs relatively low. Students fortunate enough to be offered admission typically accept, and the reasons are clear. Surrounding yourself with the best faculty, students, and institutional resources in the world is more than a dream come true. It's an offer you can hardly refuse.

2

THE PUBLIC IVIES

"With my grades and extracurricular activities, I was able to get into my top five choices. When I chose William and Mary, a few of my family members thought I did so because of the tuition savings. To be honest, I never even considered costs. I chose it because it is in my opinion the best school in the country."

Tristan
College of William and Mary

CLUES

They Might *Not* Be for You

1

You're hoping to perfect that Boston accent you've been working on since you first saw *Good Will Hunting*.

2

You thumb your nose at schools founded in the nineteenth century.

3

You'll just die if 90 percent of your classmates don't come from places you've never been.

4

You want to be a small fish in a very expensive pond.

5

You'd prefer that all those tax dollars your family has paid for public education in your state will go to someone else.

6

You consider *frugality* to be near the bottom of your personal attributes.

7

You've bought four pairs of shoes, and they match only Harvard Crimson.

8

You prefer to pay for more than what you get.

9

You suffer from bibliophobia (a fear of books).

10

Word association: someone says "public," you say "enemy."

If you dream of attending a highly selective college with state-of-the-art facilities and world-class instruction but dread the thought of dishing out a small fortune in tuition, you still have some great options. Among the nation's most competitive schools is a select group of public schools informally known as the Public Ivies. These colleges attract outstanding faculty, produce superb graduates, and offer access to excellent facilities. Like the Ivy League schools, many have billion-dollar endowments. And at least one is older than every Ivy League college except Harvard.

The Public Ivies do their jobs so well that you might have some difficulty convincing your friends and family that they're actually state supported. Your fellow graduates, however, probably already know how good a state college can be. More and more of the nation's brightest students are choosing to attend these top public schools, even when accepted by an Ivy League college.

At a Glance

There's a good reason they're known as the Public Ivies: even though they're public, they are still among the most selective schools in the world. Read on to see if one of these Public Ivies is right for you.

1. Selectivity

Many students mistakenly consider their in-state public universities as "fallback" choices or safety schools, but don't be fooled into thinking that public schools accept just anyone. Many public universities turn away far more applicants than the Ivy League schools. UCLA, with a 23 percent acceptance rate, sends rejection letters to approximately 35,000 students each year. By comparison, Harvard denies admission to roughly 17,000 students annually.

To gain admission to a Public Ivy, you'll need stellar grades, superior test scores, and a strong high school finish. This is especially true for nonresidents, who are competing for a limited number of spots at most public universities. For example, while UCLA's admission rate of 23 percent is somewhat higher than Ivy League schools such as Brown and Dartmouth, only 7 percent of those students come from out of state. For nonresidents, the

10

Public Ivies

1
University of California, Berkeley

2
University of Florida

3
University of Michigan

4
University of North Carolina

5
University of Virginia

6
University of California, Los Angeles

7
Binghamton University, State University of New York

8
University of Washington

9
Cornell University (Schools of Agriculture, Human Ecology and Industrial/Labor Relations only)

10
College of William and Mary (Virginia)

Public Ivies are just as selective—and sometimes more selective—than the true Ivy League colleges.

2. Reputation

If you're looking for a school with a stellar reputation, look no further—the Public Ivies have reputation to spare. The University of Washington, for example, counts among its faculty five Nobel Prize winners, nine MacArthur fellows, and forty members of the National Academy of Sciences. In certain disciplines, particularly among the fields of science, engineering, and medicine, these public universities actually outpace the Ivy League in terms of reputation. If you consider overall reputation to include quality of campus living, investment in graduate school research, and success on the ball field, then the Public Ivies truly stand alone at the top of the hill.

Another factor to consider is personal connections. No one holds a college in higher esteem than an alumnus, and on a headcount basis alone, the Public Ivy alumni considerably outnumber the Ivy League graduates. Don't underestimate the value of a strong alumni network when it comes time to look for a job.

3. Cost

When deciding whether a Public Ivy is right for you, you'll be considering, among other things, the price tag. Because these schools are public, you'll find they charge lower tuition rates than the Ivy League schools. But the published tuition price alone doesn't tell the whole story. Public schools typically have two price tags: one for students from in state and another, usually much higher, price tag for students from out of state. So although these colleges can be top-notch bargains for state residents, tuition for nonresidents can sometimes come close to that of the Ivy League schools.

Resident tuition at the University of Florida is less than $3,000 annually. Nonresidents, on the other hand, pay nearly $16,000 per year.

If you're a student with a high level of financial need, you might find that the Ivy League colleges can offer you a better bargain, since many will meet your entire cost through scholarships. The state schools don't have that luxury, and they generally give out much less per student in terms of financial aid. In short, don't assume that you'll always pay less by attending a public school. As anyone who's bought a car will tell you, there's much more to cost than the sticker price.

4. Academics

When it comes to academics, the Public Ivies take a backseat to no one. First-year retention rates consistently remain above 90 percent at each of these schools, and the student bodies bring impressive academic records. Both the University of Florida and University of Virginia student bodies, for example, recently had average GPAs over 3.9 and average SAT scores exceeding 1300 (on the "old" SAT). The University of California–Berkeley has even more to boast about:

- 139 Guggenheim fellows
- 221 Academy of Arts and Sciences fellows
- 3 Pulitzer Prize winners
- 7 faculty recipients of the Nobel Prize

Academic choice also weighs heavily in the Public Ivies' favor: their selection of majors is generally large and varied. The University of Michigan, for example, offers over 200 undergraduate majors. If you think you might want to study a relatively obscure field, a large public university is the only way to go.

On the downside, large public universities can sometimes lack the close intimacy typified by the Ivy League schools, and students often complain about feeling lost in the system. Other common complaints include extremely large class sizes, particularly in the first two years of enrollment; courses taught by teaching assistants instead of full professors; and a grading system that focuses too heavily on test scores and bell curves, and not enough on meaningful learning.

5. Campus Life

Campus life at the Public Ivies varies considerably from the true Ivy League colleges. Many of these universities enroll more than 25,000 students, making them entire cities unto themselves. For many students, these colleges represent the best of both worlds: a high level of academics and access to an enormous social scene. If you see yourself as outgoing and feel the need to meet as many new people as you possibly can in the next four years, this might be the right choice for you.

Athletics can also dominate these campuses to a much higher degree than the Ivy League colleges. The University of Florida, UCLA, and the University of Michigan are perennial powerhouses in NCAA football, and the University of North Carolina basketball team almost always plays deep into March Madness. Providing a varied campus life has also served these schools well in terms of alumni loyalty: alumni give back to their colleges in record amounts. Even the smallest of these schools, the College of William and Mary, has an endowment of over $350 million, evidence that graduates from these colleges believe in the choice they made.

6. Residential Life

Generally, housing at the Public Ivies is no different from that of the other large state schools described in Chapter 3. Some schools, such as the University of Virginia and William and Mary, require first-year students to live on campus. Beyond that, the larger universities usually have a lower percentage of on-campus residents than the Ivy League schools. And because these schools enroll so many students, getting the dorm of your first choice can be quite a challenge, so you'll need to apply for housing early.

The University of Michigan has over 900 student organizations.

"I had the option of living off-campus, so I did, thinking I would save money. However, because I didn't consider utilities, transportation, and the need for furniture, my off-campus costs were actually a lot higher. Plus, I felt really isolated from campus life."

Kat
University of Michigan

10

Championship Seasons

1

1991: Washington wins NCAA Football Championship

2

1995: UCLA wins NCAA Basketball Championship

3

1996: Florida wins NCAA Football Championship

4

1997: Michigan wins NCAA Football Championship

5

1998: Florida wins Women's NCAA Soccer Championship

6

2000: UCLA wins NCAA Women's Gymnastics Championship

7

2003: North Carolina wins Women's NCAA Soccer Championship

8

2004: California wins NCAA Men's Golf Championship

9

2004: Virginia wins Women's NCAA Lacrosse Championship

10

2005: North Carolina wins NCAA Basketball Championship

The benefits of living in a residence hall, particularly during your first year, usually outweigh the drawbacks. In addition to helping to build a sense of community, living on campus will help you avoid the off-campus headaches of commuting and parking, and you'll avoid potentially reduced access to educational resources, libraries, and recreation facilities.

7. Atmosphere

If you choose to apply to a Public Ivy, you'll find an extremely diverse array of choices in terms of size, location, and climate. If your ideal Christmas tree has palm leaves, UCLA and the University of Florida will keep you warm throughout the year. Likewise, if the thought of 10,000 screaming football fans horrifies you, tiny William and Mary might be just what the doctor ordered. On the downside, many students who choose a Public Ivy do so because of cost considerations, which essentially means that you have only one option: your in-state college. If you live in Texas, for example, and decide to attend the University of Virginia, you'll pay $22,000 in tuition. And gaining state residency solely for the purpose of paying in-state tuition is not allowed.

Excluding the issue of cost, however, the Public Ivies can be exciting places to study, with calendars full of activities, festivals, and sporting events. The campus populations often have an international flavor, attracting students and faculty from all over the world. Few students will ever claim that these campuses are boring places to live, and this big-college experience is part of the reason these schools are so popular. Just as many people want to move to the big city, many students are attracted to the excitement of a place with so many people, activities, and academic options.

A word of caution: all this hustle and bustle can be overwhelming for new students. If you do ultimately choose a Public Ivy, try to not to waste all those academic resources. If possible, enroll in an honors college to try to keep your class sizes small.

8. Students

The students who choose the Public Ivies come with impressive résumés. In addition to the stellar classes of the Universities of Florida and Virginia, the 2002 incoming class at UCLA had a weighted average of 4.11. But students at

10

FAMOUS
Public Ivy Alums

1

UC Berkeley: Steve Wozniak

2

University of Florida: Bob Vila

3

University of Michigan: James Earl Jones

4

University of North Carolina: Mia Hamm

5

University of Virginia: Thurgood Marshall

6

UCLA: Michelle Kwan

7

SUNY Binghamton: Camille Paglia

8

University of Washington: Bruce Lee

9

College of William and Mary: Thomas Jefferson

10

Miami University of Ohio: Rita Dove

state schools, even the Public Ivies, can seem much more like ordinary Janes and Joes than what you might find at a super-pricey elite college.

That certainly doesn't mean you should relax in the classroom, however. With large universities come large class sizes, more limited time with professors, and more competition for precious resources. True, in terms of numbers, the Public Ivies produce as many top fellowship winners as their Ivy League counterparts, but on a percentage basis, the smaller, private schools have a clear advantage. You'll need to work hard to stand out.

9. Professors

Like the students who choose a Public Ivy, the professors are among the most talented in the nation. Many are graduates of an Ivy League college but have chosen to teach in a large public university because of the unparalleled resources often found there. The affection is mutual. Public universities heavily recruit the best professors for their ability to produce research, bring in grant money, and add to the list of faculty publications.

Unfortunately, new students may not reap the benefits of all this academic expertise. When professors at public universities feel pressured to publish, they often rely on teaching assistants to lead classes. Even if you sign up for a class with a big-shot professor, you may find that you only see him or her once a week in a large lecture hall. You might feel like you're attending a concert rather than a class.

When talking to admissions counselors at a Public Ivy, be sure and ask specific questions.

- Will you be guaranteed close faculty contact or relegated to the back of a lecture hall?

State college students are not all about grades, and one of the reasons many graduating high school seniors choose a public university is because of the down-to-earth factor.

Many professors are pressured to write books and articles in addition to carrying out their regular teaching responsibilities. Students at these "publish or perish" colleges often feel like their needs are being overlooked because professors are focused mainly on their own research. In many cases, professors who do not publish hurt their career, status, or potential for advancement.

- Will you get your first shot at classes led by the professors you want, or will a twenty-one-year-old grad student be the link between you and your future?

You may want to consider a smaller alternative if the Public Ivy of your first choice cannot reasonably assure you access to what may have been the number-one reason you chose the school to begin with.

10. The Intangibles

If you have a superior academic record, an outgoing nature, and an aversion to paying $30,000 for tuition, then a Public Ivy could be the perfect choice for you. It could be an especially good choice if you manage to arrange small class sizes, seek out close interaction with full professors, and aren't easily sidetracked by the numerous distractions that come from lots of students and activities. Public or not, these schools can potentially offer an education to match any in the world.

If you apply to one of these schools, you should find out from the admissions officer what steps you need to take to maximize your learning opportunities. Some schools, for example, allow you to apply to honors colleges within the university, which usually guarantees smaller class sizes and one-on-one contact with faculty.

Don't forget to consider the amount of time you'll need to graduate from one of these public schools. Many students blow a great tuition deal by taking longer than four years to earn their degree. Many public college students actually take *six years or more* to finish their education. Try to find out how the Public Ivy of your choice performs in this area. Four-year graduation rates of at least 60 percent exist at some schools, including:

- University of North Carolina
- University of Virginia
- College of William and Mary
- SUNY Binghamton

Is This the Right Choice?

Depending on what you're looking for, a Public Ivy might be the perfect choice, particularly if you live in the right state. Residents of Michigan, Washington, California, New York, Florida, North Carolina, and Virginia are all intimately familiar with the quality of their tax-supported universities. They are also well aware of the bargain they can receive by paying up to $25,000 less in tuition each year than what the private Ivy League colleges charge for the same quality of education.

Even if you don't live in one of these states, out-of-state tuition rates are still around $10,000 cheaper than Ivy League sticker prices. Nonresidents are also attracted to the possibility of being able to root for a national football or basketball powerhouse, choose from a vast number of student clubs, and be a part of a vibrant and exciting campus.

And size truly does matter: with just a couple of exceptions, the Public Ivies dwarf their private counterparts. The largest Ivy League school, Cornell University, has 14,000 students, many of which are, in fact, part of Cornell's public branch. The largest of the Public Ivies, the University of Florida, has over twice that many students, with an enrollment of almost 34,000 students. So these colleges make good choices if you seek a high level of instruction *and* a big-college experience.

3

STATE SCHOOLS

"I thought about a private college, but in the end, no school offered as many programs as my state's university. Plus, it's close to home and won't leave me with $20,000 in loan debt. I know I made the right choice."

Naya
University of Colorado

CLUES

They Might *Not* Be for You

1

You prefer to be at least six months older than your teacher.

2

You avoid schools that pay the football coach more than the college president.

3

The thought of running into your high school classmates makes you break out into a rash.

4

You want to be a big fish in a small pond.

5

You prefer ivy to just about every plant in the whole, wide world.

6

You're convinced that it's impossible to get more than what you've paid for.

7

Your hometown just isn't big enough for those stellar SAT scores.

8

You live in Wyoming and want more than one choice.

9

You suffer from enochlophobia (a fear of crowds).

10

Word association: someone says "state," you say "confusion."

State schools are publicly supported institutions of higher education. Every state has its own college system, which usually falls under the title of "University of (insert state name here)." These colleges receive much of their operating support through tax dollars, and, as a result, their tuition is considerably lower than most private schools. Plus, since these colleges can be quite large, they have a tremendous number of resources, in terms of both facilities and personnel.

The flagship universities, which we'll focus on here, represent the largest and most comprehensive schools in the country. They typically enroll more students than any other four-year colleges and are the focal points of the educational system within their states. This means that they receive the lion's share of resources, publicity, and money. They often have outstanding athletic programs to complement a massive number of degree options.

Because they are so large, the flagship universities are often broken down into smaller units, usually known as colleges. Rutgers University, the flagship of New Jersey, for example, has several specialty colleges within its system, such as Rutgers College, a liberal arts school, and the Mason Gross School of the Arts. If you want to carve out your own niche with small class sizes but still want to feel part of a larger community, attending a small college within a flagship system may be the way to go.

At a Glance

Just as you may get an instant picture in your mind when someone says "Ivy League," you probably have some preconceived ideas of what a state school is like, and whether it's the right choice for you. State schools come with their own unique set of characteristics, and the following 10 things will give you the lowdown about these gentle giants of higher education.

1. Selectivity

Though not quite as selective as the Ivy League colleges (with the exception of the 10 "Public Ivies" listed in Chapter 2), the flagship universities do not offer admission to just anyone. Many receive over 15,000 applicants each year, so deciding to apply to a public college shouldn't lead you to slack off your final semester of high school. In fact, even those public universities not considered "elite" still manage to attract extremely bright students. Roughly half of Penn State University students graduated in the top 10 percent of their classes, and the University of Texas counts over 50 National Merit Scholars among its most recent freshman class.

2. Reputation

Reputation ranges considerably from one flagship to the next, though they generally hold the title of most prestigious public college within their respective states. The flagship universities also do a terrific job of recruiting extremely qualified faculty members, who are attracted to the tremendous facilities and resources that few colleges beyond the flagships manage to provide.

The reputation of each flagship university also varies by the individual departments within. The Journalism School within the University of Missouri, for example, is far more selective than the university as a whole. In fact, you'll probably have to complete two applications to many of these schools, one to the university and one to the individual college in which you'd like to study.

3. Cost

The University of Texas system has an endowment of over $10 billion, the third largest in the nation, behind only Harvard and Yale.

For in-state residents, the flagship universities typically cost a little more than the other public colleges, but most still charge less than $8,000 per year, making these highly economical options. Additionally, the flagship universities tend to have the largest endowments (funds raised by an institution outside of tuition and tax support), so if you have outstanding credentials, you can likely bring these costs down even lower through scholarships.

For nonresidents, the flagship universities will typically charge a little more than the branch campuses or other state colleges. Nevertheless, you will still probably pay less to attend an out-of-state public flagship university than you would pay to attend a private college of similar stature. And as with in-state residents, you will likely reduce those costs even further if you have an outstanding academic record and are able to win scholarships.

4. Academics

Though many flagship universities may have stellar reputations, they are infamous for sacrificing undergraduate teaching in favor of faculty research and graduate studies. Freshmen and sophomores, in particular, often complain about being assigned to extremely large classes, sometimes taught by teaching assistants instead of professors. Teaching assistants are typically graduate students, and, though they are sometimes excellent, they rarely have the relevant qualifications needed to teach at the local elementary or middle school.

If you decide that a flagship university lies in your future, you should find out from the admissions office how many classes are led by teaching assistants. Bargain or not, if you are attracted to a university because of the reputation of its faculty, you owe it to yourself to actually learn directly from those professors in the field of your choice. If the college cannot offer you assurances on how to avoid this bait and switch, you might want to consider another college option.

5. Campus Life

Talk to many students, and they'll tell you they chose to attend a flagship university based on the quality of campus life. From NCAA sports to Greek life to student activities, nobody does it bigger than the large public university

"Before classes began I was bombarded with decisions: should I go Greek, purchase a season pass to the football and basketball games, sign up for Amnesty International, and on and on. For a moment, I nearly forgot that the reason I came was to earn a degree."

Terrence
Penn State

"The admissions counselor sold me on the idea that the university had the best teachers in the country. Not that I would know. All my classes during the first year were taught by graduate students. I felt like it was a huge waste of my tuition dollars."

Anonymous

system. If you've ever dreamed of attending a homecoming football game with over 50,000 adoring fans or running for class president of a student body larger than your hometown, this may be the right choice.

Even for the most outgoing students, the sheer number of campus activities can sometimes prove overwhelming. With hundreds of extracurricular options from which to choose, your biggest challenges will be selecting the right activities . . . and not letting them get in the way of your studies.

6. Residential Life

Not long ago, colleges placed relatively little emphasis on the quality of their dormitories. However, more and more studies are showing the link between student retention and student satisfaction, so residential life has received much more attention. The large universities have tried hard to overcome the negative stereotypes of living on campus (nightmarish roommates, Lilliputian-sized rooms, and stomach-turning food) by transforming plain old dormitories into full-service residence halls, complete with full-time student support staff, tutoring and wellness centers, and chefs unafraid to eat their own creations. Some, like the University of Minnesota, have even created special "Living and Learning" communities to integrate academics with residential life.

The trick for you will be to get the real scoop on residential life. If you do choose a large public university, make sure you understand that the sample dorm they may show you on your student tour will likely represent the best possible room, not necessarily what you'll wind up with. With so many students, competition for the best living spaces will be more intense here that at any other type of college.

Dorm Life: 10 Amenities You May Find Next Door

1. Student support staff
2. Tutoring services
3. Wellness center
4. Dining hall
5. Computer center
6. Student gym and rec center
7. Laundry room
8. Career planning and placement office
9. Academic advising
10. Volunteer and community service office

7. Atmosphere

With thousands of students, vast campuses, and the prevalence of teaching assistants and large classrooms, it's no wonder that many freshmen complain that the big universities can seem a bit impersonal. Texas A&M University alone has a campus of over 5,200 acres and 100 buildings. This probably isn't the right choice for you if you imagine the ideal experience to be one where you are on a first-name basis with the college president.

On the other hand, if you have a "bigger is better" mentality and want access to as many opportunities and as many people as possible, you really have few other choices beyond a large public university. Like all types of colleges, the flagships have their drawbacks. Being boring isn't one of them.

8. Students

Students at state schools are a true study in contrasts. On one end of the spectrum you have truly outstanding academic performers who go on to win prestigious fellowships in numbers that equal the elite colleges. The state schools have redoubled their efforts in recent years to recruit the best high school graduates with hefty financial aid incentives.

On the other hand, state schools, particularly the ultralarge mega-universities, can also provide havens for underachieving students who are able to disappear in three-hundred-student lectures. Students at some of these

LARGEST
State Schools

1

Ohio State University: 50,995 students

2

University of Minnesota: 50,954

3

University of Texas at Austin: 50,377

4

Arizona State University: 49,171

5

University of Florida: 47,933

6

Michigan State University: 44,836

7

Texas A & M University: 44,435

8

Penn State University: 41,289

9

University of Wisconsin: 41,169

10

University of Illinois: 40,360

schools are infamous for hiring note takers, buying previous quizzes, and skipping class until test time.

If you decide that a state college is right for you, don't let yourself get lackadaisical in your studies. Try to get into an honor's program that offers smaller class sizes and closer interaction with professors. Don't let yourself get into a habit of skipping classes, since it can be a hard cycle to break. And don't try to be your own academic advisor, since state school students are well-known for taking more than four years to graduate: the drive to finish college is perhaps less urgent since tuition costs so much less than at a private university.

9. Professors

Some of the brightest academicians in the world make up the faculties of state colleges, bringing needed prestige, awards, and grant money to underfunded public schools. But all of these qualifications sometimes come at a cost to students. When state schools load professors with both research responsibilities and large class sizes, the result can be a lack of meaningful interaction between teacher and student. Many lower-level classes are actually led by teaching assistants, who often lack the education or knowledge to effectively lead new students through their coursework.

Many state colleges employ a grading system that relies heavily on a bell curve. Instructors often feel so pressured to create student-learning outcomes that meet the norm that they assign grades along a statistical formula that predetermines how many students will get A's and how many will get D's. Students usually find out about the "curve" quickly, and the result can be a competitive and uncaring classroom focused entirely on not getting the lowest score on any given test.

There have been 21 total Rhodes Scholars from the University of California–Berkeley and 7 Truman Scholars from Oklahoma State University in the past eight years, and there were 29 Fulbright Fellows from the University of Michigan in 2003.

10 THINGS

About Branch Campuses

---

1   Not all branch campuses offer guaranteed admission, so don't automatically assume that your local state college will be a safety school.

2   Branch campuses will not score very highly among the most common ranking systems, but reputation can be highly subjective.

3   Branch campuses offer tremendous tuition deals for in-state residents.

4   Since the branch campuses usually enroll fewer students, you're much less likely to suffer through large lectures led by teaching assistants.

5   Professors usually have much less pressure to conduct research, leaving them more time to focus on undergraduate teaching.

6   Many flagship universities have made it even easier for students to transfer in for their final two years of college.

7   Even if you don't transfer, you may still have access to the flagship resources, including libraries and laboratories.

8   Branch campuses come in all shapes, sizes, and settings.

9   Though some branch campuses don't have dorms, the vast majority do.

10 Students often have genuine pride in their local schools.

If you decide to attend a state school, try to get into an honor's program that will allow you to take advantage of the outstanding faculty. Even better, take a look at a state school that supplements its letter grades with narrative evaluations. The Evergreen State College, the New School of Florida, and the University of California at Santa Cruz are examples of state schools that go the extra mile when it comes to providing meaningful grades to their students.

10. The Intangibles

Large state schools can resemble small cities, with thousands of students, teachers, and staff mingling among hundreds of degree programs. Campus life brings even more hustle and bustle, with Greek life, intercollegiate athletics, and student activities dominating your out-of-class time. At those schools where enrollment exceeds 15,000, many new students can feel lost in this sea of excitement.

But state schools can also be quite intimate, some with enrollments not much larger than your high school. In other words, state schools offer a tremendous diversity of characteristics. Whatever you're looking for, you will likely find at least one good public school alternative, even if you've considered only private colleges.

Perhaps because of the longstanding stereotypes of flagships as impersonal colleges focused more on research than undergraduate teaching, the large public universities have become pioneers in the field of the first-year experience. A good example is the University of South Carolina, home of the National Research Center for First-Year Experience and Students in Transition. By offering for-credit classes on how to adjust to college life as well as staff support for everything from academic advising to career counseling, students receive the best of both

Other Large Campuses

Are you interested in a large campus feel but want a private school experience? Several large private colleges may meet your needs, including Brigham Young University, Syracuse, DePaul, Baylor, and the Rochester Institute of Technology, each with over 10,000 students.

worlds: a large campus experience with a personal touch. The key for you, should you decide to attend a large university, will be to take advantage of that support.

Attending a branch campus of a state school also has its unique benefits. Classes led by professors, access to world-class facilities, and a chance to be a big fish in a small pond: these are a few of the reasons a branch campus might be the right choice for you. Hidden college treasures may be found right in your own backyard.

The Branch Campuses

The main public university systems often have several associated branch campuses and/or state colleges separate from the main flagship university. Texas and New York each have over thirty public four-year colleges and universities from which to choose, and several other states have a dozen or more. If you want to earn your degree close to home, you will likely find a good, affordable option at one of these state schools.

You should by no means consider these schools as "second best" options. The branch campuses and state colleges are probably a lot more diverse than you think, ranging from massive research universities to tiny liberal arts colleges. The University of California at Davis, for example, has a 5,300-acre campus with over 30,000 students and each year receives over $400 million in research funding, making it one of the top universities in the country. Looking for something a little cozier? The New College of Florida is one of the smallest (fewer than 700 undergrads) and most difficult public schools to gain admission to (53 percent acceptance rate).

These schools offer a host of other benefits as well, and some of the smaller branch campuses, in true underdog fashion, have begun to challenge their bigger counterparts on all levels.

Is This the Right Choice?

Whether you choose a flagship university or a small branch campus, state schools offer many benefits that make them perennial favorites among the college-going public. These colleges are definitely the place to be in terms of action. Big lecture halls, big social activities, and big campus events all add to the feeling of excitement. But take care that all these opportunities don't distract from your studies: memories of a football championship will mean very little if you never earn your degree.

Even if you attend one of the smaller branch campuses, you may still have access to the resources of the entire university system. The large state universities offer just about every class you can imagine and almost limitless access to state-of-the-art facilities. If you want to learn journalism at a real television station or nursing at a real hospital, large state universities can give you those opportunities.

An Easy Decision

If you live in Wyoming and want to attend a public four-year university, you have an easy decision ahead of you: the University of Wyoming is the only public four-year college in the state.

4
LIBERAL ARTS SCHOOLS

"After everything I had heard about college—large lecture halls, stand-offish professors, and cookie-cutter quizzes—I was shocked to talk with teachers and students who genuinely seemed to care about learning. I can't imagine settling for anything less."

Ben
Gonzaga University

CLUES

They Might *Not* Be for You

1

The thought of sharing your ideas in class gives you chills.

2

You have a lifelong devotion to multiple-choice tests.

3

You already bought four year's worth of number 2 pencils.

4

You rank *cooperation* somewhere near the top of your pet peeves.

5

You're looking to be a small fish in a big pond.

6

You're hoping to blend in among three hundred students during Chemistry 101.

7

You have high hopes your college football team will make it to a bowl game.

8

Having a professor call you by name sends you to your "happy place."

9

You suffer from sophophobia (a fear of learning).

10

Word association: someone says "liberal," you say "conservative."

President James Garfield once remarked, "The ideal college is Mark Hopkins on one end of a log and a student on the other." This quote represents the idea that a college education should consist of students and teachers working closely together in an attitude of openness and communication. Liberal arts colleges believe that developing critical learning skills and fostering intellectual curiosity are even more important than selecting a major.

Some liberal arts colleges don't even have majors. Or grades. Or arbitrary course requirements. And if the thought of a lecture hall with four hundred students learning rote material frightens you, then liberal arts colleges will probably think you're a good candidate for admission.

At a Glance

The best liberal arts colleges share the following characteristics:

- Small class sizes
- Close working relationships with fellow students and faculty
- Emphasis on developing solid speaking and writing skills

Whereas much of your high school education probably focused on memorization and regurgitation of knowledge, a liberal arts education focuses on why that knowledge is important. Read on to see what else makes liberal arts schools unique.

1. Selectivity

There are over 200 liberal arts colleges, and many are among the most highly selective schools in the country.

"In my first class, I was stunned to see a student raise her hand to actually disagree with the professor. And instead of banishing her, he encouraged her to present her opinion. I knew I had found the right school for me."

Taylor
Carleton College

GREAT

Private Liberal Arts Colleges

1

Swarthmore College (Pennsylvania)

2

Williams College (Massachusetts)

3

Pomona College (California)

4

Grinnell College (Iowa)

5

Middlebury College (Vermont)

6

Carleton College (Minnesota)

7

Bowdoin College (Maine)

8

Davidson College (North Carolina)

9

Manhattanville College (New York)

10

Oberlin College (Ohio)

Schools such as Oberlin College and Swarthmore College offer highly regarded liberal arts educations and admit just a small percentage of applicants. Amherst College admits only 18 percent of students who apply. Wellesley College admits slightly more, but only because fewer people can apply: Wellesley is an all-women's college.

If you seek the benefits of a private liberal arts college, you'll find some good schools with higher acceptance rates, such as Grinnell College in Iowa, Trinity College in Connecticut, and Kenyon College in Ohio. A few, such as Presbyterian College in South Carolina, Lewis and Clark College in Oregon, and DePauw University in Indiana, actually accept the majority of applicants, making them terrific safety schools (if they're not already among your top choices).

2. Reputation

Many of the most prestigious colleges in the country are liberal arts schools. A school's reputation stems in large part from the quality of its teaching, and professors who truly love meaningful interaction with students choose liberal arts colleges time and again. But a school also owes its reputation to the kinds of students it attracts, and each year some of the brightest students in the country choose to study at a liberal arts college. For example, Barnard College in New York has a freshman class with an average GPA of 3.93, and at Carleton College in Minnesota, 16 percent of incoming freshmen are National Merit Scholars each year.

The reputations of liberal arts colleges tend to vary by region. While many students and families in the South may have never heard of Whitman College in Walla Walla, Washington, employers in the Pacific Northwest eagerly hire any graduates who don't decide to go on to medical, law, or business school. Likewise, many in Seattle may be unfamiliar with Wofford College in Spartanburg, South Carolina, but Wofford has an equally strong network of friends and alumni in the South. If prestige is an important factor to you in determining which college to choose, make sure you look at both national and local reputations.

3. Cost

Running a private college committed to small class sizes without the benefit of state tax support costs money. For this reason, the tuition at liberal arts colleges is usually much higher than tuition at research universities, and sometimes even more than the tuition at Ivy League schools. You'll have to pay particular attention to your financial aid award when applying to a private liberal arts college. Fortunately, many of these schools have significant endowments, which allow them to grant enough financial aid to meet your need.

There are some affordable options if you decide a liberal arts college is right for you. Centre College in Kentucky, for example, is a perennial best buy among the liberal arts schools with total costs (including tuition and living expenses) falling under $30,000 per year—and over 80 percent of students receive some form of financial assistance. Warren Wilson College in North Carolina is even cheaper, with tuition around $19,000. There are even better deals: Berea College in Kentucky, the College of the Ozarks in Missouri, and Deep Springs College in Nevada each offer a terrific education completely free of any tuition charges.

While private liberal arts colleges tend to charge more for tuition, they also do a much better job graduating students in four years or fewer. Many, including the University of the Pacific, even offer a four-year graduation guarantee. If you can't graduate within four years through no fault of your own, the college will pick up the tab until you do.

4. Academics

Liberal arts colleges focus on undergraduate teaching. If you were to transfer from a large university to a small liberal arts college, one of the first things you'd notice would be the difference in student-faculty relations, which are much more personal than at larger schools. Large schools can manipulate statistics to show they have a low student-to-faculty ratio, but these statistics speak only to the quantity of teachers, not the quality of teaching. Unlike at those large universities, you won't have to worry about taking classes taught by graduate student teaching assistants or sitting in the occasional lecture with over three hundred other students.

The method of instruction at liberal arts colleges is also different from larger schools. The liberal arts philosophy puts forth that students should do more than just memorize answers for a multiple-choice test. Students at these schools develop skills in reading comprehension, critical thinking, and writing—and gain a love for lifelong learning. Instead of lectures, professors lead students through seminars, classroom experiences where everyone's voice is heard and where all opinions matter. This experience can be a bit shocking for someone who's come from a school system where the teacher is always right or where students are not expected to write papers or participate in class discussions.

You might be surprised by how well liberal arts colleges train students for careers in math and science. Many liberal arts colleges actually produce a higher percentage of future doctors, scientists, and mathematicians than the top research universities. The students at private liberal arts colleges also excel in winning national and international awards. Pitzer College, for example, with less than 1,000 students, recently announced that six current students have won Fulbright Awards for 2005, a record that no major research university can match.

5. Campus Life

Few schools integrate campus life with academics better than the liberal arts colleges, which encourage learning both inside and outside the classroom. Since liberal arts colleges typically have lower enrollments, students have a greater opportunity to have meaningful interactions with one another. You'll find many of the same kinds of activities you would at a large university, such as athletics and Greek life, only on a much smaller scale.

The large universities may have campus events that reach epic proportions, such as Division I sporting events, but students at these large colleges might be best described as mere spectators of campus activities. At liberal arts colleges, students are far more likely to be active participants in campus life.

6. Residential Life

The liberal arts schools emphasize the importance of living on campus, and many will require that students, particularly first-year students and sophomores, live in the residence halls. The idea is to create a learning community where everyone participates equally.

Because of this on-campus living requirement, liberal arts colleges typically have professional student-affairs staff (or sometimes even professors) who manage residence life. Typical of liberal arts schools is the "Residential Education" program at Hobart and William Smith Colleges in Geneva, New York. The name alone implies that dormitories are much more than just a place to store your clothes, and the staff takes their mission of establishing a vital learning and living community very seriously. Students must sign a contract through which they agree to respect all community residents. If you fear the idea of a living in a dorm full of students more concerned with all-night parties than early-morning exams, this might be the place for you.

7. Atmosphere

With such small class sizes, liberal arts students will receive a high-quality education. The most reputable of the liberal arts colleges attract some of the brightest professors and staff in the world, whose focus, unlike at the "publish or perish" environments of the large universities, remains on teaching. The liberal arts campus creates an atmosphere of learning both inside and outside of the classroom, and it's not unusual for teachers and students to carry on their conversations after the proverbial bell has rung.

While there is much less of an emphasis on athletics and Greek life than at large universities, there is no sacrifice when it comes to community building. In fact, being a student at a small liberal arts college can seem analogous to living in a small town. Everyone on campus may know your name (and, more often than not, your business too), and students are often on a first-name basis with their professors—and sometimes even the college president.

8. Students

Students at the liberal arts colleges can seem mature beyond their years, many consciously choosing their school based on its ability to meet their needs. What they need is an education that stimulates their natural curiosity, fulfills their desire to interact meaningfully, and helps them become not just better educated but also more informed. Education is more than just the means to a bachelor's degree: it's a key to making the world a better place.

That said, you might find that the typical liberal arts students are a little different from their large university peers. They are often more politically, socially, and culturally active than what you might be used to. They can also take complete ownership of the classroom, unafraid to share their ideas and opinions. This combination of inquisitiveness and participation helps explain why they win admission to the best graduate schools in such large

> You could say that liberal arts students have a bit of a romantic streak: many want to make the world a better place.

10

FORTUNE 1000 CEOs
From Liberal Arts Schools

1

Janet Robinson, CEO, The New York Times Co.: Salve Regina University (Rhode Island)

2

Richard Templeton, CEO, Texas Instruments: Union College (New York)

3

Brenda Barnes, CEO, Sara Lee: Augustana College (Illinois)

4

Brian Markison, CEO, King Pharmaceuticals: Iona College (New York)

5

Elden Smith, CEO, Fleetwood Enterprises: Whittier College (California)

6

Ward Klein, CEO, Energizer: St. Olaf College (Minnesota)

7

Steven Alesio, CEO, Dun and Bradstreet: St. Francis College (New York)

8

Clarence Otis, CEO, Darden Restaurants: Williams College (Massachusetts)

9

Maggie Wilderotter, CEO, Citizens Communications: College of the Holy Cross (Massachusetts)

10

Robert DiMuccio, CEO, Amica Mutual Insurance: Providence College (Rhode Island)

numbers. This isn't to say that a quiet, introspective high school student won't thrive in a liberal arts setting—many high school students come into their own once they arrive at a liberal arts college. All it really takes is the right kind of setting for them to come alive.

9. Professors

The liberal arts colleges pretty much set the standard for teaching and learning. Not as singularly focused on research as their university peers, and not quite as self-centered as some of the "rock star" professors you might find at the Ivy Leagues, the liberal arts teachers truly live up to the example set decades ago by Mark Hopkins. The best liberal arts teachers serve as facilitators, not lecturers. They understand that each student has a talent for learning, and their job is to bring out the academic hidden deep inside you.

This explains why liberal arts colleges have set new trends in grading students. Whereas the Ivy League instructors are notorious for grade inflation, and the public university teachers are equally renowned for sticking to the bell curve, liberal arts teachers feel that grades are more than an assessment. They are a tool that should be used to help students get better. Many liberal arts colleges promote the use of narrative evaluations. Instead of or combined with letter grades, narrative evaluations allow teachers to give students in-depth feedback about their performance in the classroom.

10. The Intangibles

Many first-year students discount the importance of good teaching when choosing a college without fully understanding the benefits. Caring and committed teachers can help you both in and outside the classroom. If you're thinking about graduate school or applying for a presti-

10

GREAT

Public Liberal Arts Schools

1
Keene State College (New Hampshire)

2
Massachusetts College of Liberal Arts

3
Southern Oregon University

4
Henderson State University (Arkansas)

5
Fort Lewis College (Colorado)

6
University of Mary Washington (Virginia)

7
University of Montevallo (Alabama)

8
University of North Carolina at Asheville

9
Eastern Connecticut State University

10
Truman State University (Missouri)

gious award, solid letters of support from full professors who actually remember your name are as important as a high GPA. If you want to eventually land a job where your ideas matter, then you deserve a classroom experience that offers the same. If you feel like the best learning experience promotes cooperation among students instead of competition, then you're in luck: this is one of the underlying philosophies of liberal arts education. Elements like these can't be boiled down into a flashy brochure, but if these are your values, a private liberal arts college might be the way to go.

Public liberal arts colleges offer a great compromise for students who want a personal education at a low cost. These are also good choices for commuting students who are looking for a more intense classroom experience but don't necessarily want it to carry over into their student activities or home life. For this reason, you might find more age diversity at public liberal arts colleges, as older students generally prefer a more inclusive classroom than they can find at a large university, while preferring to live off-campus (something dissuaded at the small private schools).

The things you *won't* find at the typical liberal arts college—large lecture halls, endless multiple-choice examinations, and teaching assistants instead of actual professors—speak volumes about why these colleges are both popular and effective, attracting and producing some of the brightest students in the country.

Is This the Right Choice?

If you come to find that a liberal arts college suits your needs, you'll be happy to know that you'll have a wide range of choices. Liberal arts colleges can be found in

Other Options

Want a liberal arts experience at a public school cost? Many state schools offer affordable, and life-changing, options. Some admit the majority of student applicants, so selectivity isn't an issue.

every region of the country, in both rural and metropolitan settings, and include both private and public institutions. Some large universities even offer liberal arts education within their colleges or departments, so students who want both a big-campus feel and small-classroom setting can get their way too.

Liberal arts colleges are definitely not the place to go if you're hoping to blend in with the crowd or learn a very specific and highly technical trade, such as engineering or nursing. These institutions focus on critical thinking and lifelong learning, which may explain why such a high percentage of liberal arts students go on to graduate, medical, or law school.

Graduates from these schools will likely tell you that their liberal arts education changed their lives for the better, even if they don't immediately land a high-paying job. If you desire highly interactive classes where your thoughts and opinions really matter, a liberal arts college could be what you're looking for.

FINE ARTS SCHOOLS

"I almost felt bad for my friends as they tried to decide which college to attend. As a musician, I never had to think twice. There was never any doubt I would go to Berklee."

Phil
Berklee College of Music

CLUES
They Might *Not* Be for You

1

Your primary focus is earning a practical degree and
not improving your art.

2

You don't remember ever hearing your parents say,
"Even my kid could paint that."

3

Degree or not, you don't believe it's possible to make a living as an artist.

4

You rank *artistic* near the bottom of your personal attributes.

5

You think Koi ponds are too showy.

6

You prefer your teachers to remain behind the podium.

7

Performing in front of an audience sends you to your "happy place."

8

You want to continue your mastery of multiple-choice tests.

9

You suffer from chorophobia (a fear of dancing).

10

Word association: someone says "art," you say "critic."

More than any other kind of college, the fine arts schools encourage imagination and a recognition of beauty, whether it be in poetry, painting, performance, drawing, photography, printmaking, sculpture, theatre, or opera. Many fine arts students say that their decision to attend one of these schools was never a matter of choice: they felt a calling to be an artist, and attending a fine arts school was a natural next step.

Students at these colleges typically earn a Bachelor's of Fine Arts (BFA). Graduates can then go on to additional schooling, such as earning a Master's of Fine Arts (MFA), or enter the workforce. While many fine arts students do go on to successful independent careers as artists, more and more are being recruited by corporate America to add a little style to their businesses. With the growing importance of the internet in business competition, many fine arts grads are finding themselves as web-artists-in-residence at large corporations.

At a Glance

If you seek a fine arts education, you won't have to look very far to find a school. But before you start sending off applications, you need to know the whole story. Applying to a fine arts college means you're making a serious commitment to a type of education that may not easily transfer back to a traditional school should you decide later on that you want to pursue a different path.

1. Selectivity

Only a relatively few fine arts schools can be classified as highly selective. Juilliard, for example, accepts only around 10 percent of student applicants. A few more, such as the Lyme Academy College of Fine Arts, Otis College of Art + Design, and Corcoran College of Art and Design, accept roughly half of applicants. But by and large, fine arts schools usually accept the majority of applicants. Despite this openness, these schools generally have small student bodies, partly due to the fact that fine arts colleges often have some of the lowest retention rates of any kind of college in the country.

The advantage to the near-universal open-door admissions policies is that you have much more freedom in picking the school that's right for you.

10

GREAT

Fine Arts Schools

1
Savannah College of Art and Design

2
North Carolina School of the Arts, Winston-Salem

3
Juilliard School, New York City

4
Berklee College of Music, Boston

5
Cornish College of the Arts, Seattle

6
University of the Arts, Philadelphia

7
Otis College of Art + Design, Los Angeles

8
School of the Art Institute of Chicago

9
Kansas City Art Institute

10
Cleveland Institute of Art

You'll very likely receive acceptance letters from most, if not all, of the fine arts colleges to which you apply. You'll have the luxury of exploring the finer aspects of each college when making your decision.

2. Reputation

Fine arts colleges in America are known around the world for producing talented graduates. The Berklee College of Music, for example, has such a good reputation internationally that 26 percent of its student body comes from foreign nations, more than any other college in the country.

As an artist, your success will have much more to do with your body of work than the name of the college on your degree. For this reason, the few "elite" schools among fine arts institutions differ greatly from traditional elite colleges in that they actually graduate a relatively small number of students. A world-class artist doesn't necessarily need a degree to make a living. Reputation counts much more for students who are interested in continuing their education in a master's program or who wish to use their artistic training in a regular career. You should ask an admissions counselor to provide information about where graduates wind up and how many get into their graduate school of first choice.

You should be aware that there are a fair share of for-profit "art schools" that are not accredited to grant degrees or offer federal financial aid. Make sure that you ask for an art school's accreditation before sending in any application fees. Unfortunately, many of these schools have names that sound very similar to fully accredited colleges, so it may be hard to tell without a little investigation.

You should be able to uncover accreditation information from the school's website. If the website is a "dot com," as opposed to a "dot edu," it's likely a private business.

GREAT
Arts Awards and Fellowships

1

Guggenheim Fellowship: average $35,000

2

Whiting Writer's Awards: $35,000

3

National Endowment for the Arts Literature Fellowship: $20,000

4

Lila Wallace Reader's Digest Fund: $35,000

5

American Academy of Arts and Letters Awards: up to $75,000

6

Katherine Anne Porter Award: $20,000

7

Harold D. Vursell Award: $10,000

8

Benjamin Danks Award: $20,000

9

Nicholl Fellowships in Screenwriting: up to $30,000

10

ARTS Awards for Young Artists: up to $10,000

3. Cost

The costs for a fine arts school vary. If you attend a public fine arts school as a state resident, your tuition will be fairly low. In-state residents pay less than $5,000 per year in tuition at the North Carolina School of the Arts in Winston-Salem. In-state residents at the Massachusetts College of Art don't pay much more, around $6,500. Nonresidents, however, will pay over twice that at both schools.

Paying out-of-state tuition at a public fine arts school may still be a more affordable option than going the private route. Several private fine arts colleges, including the Otis College of Art + Design in Los Angeles and the School of the Art Institute of Chicago, charge over $25,000 per year in tuition and fees. Tuition at the majority of private fine arts schools averages around $20,000. A few private schools are much more reasonable: the Memphis College of Art and the Laguna College of Art and Design, for example, each charge around $16,000 per year.

For-profit businesses calling themselves "art schools" may charge substantially less than a fully accredited private fine arts college, but because they cannot award federal aid, such as Pell Grants or Stafford Loans, you might wind up paying more in the long run. Attending a nonaccredited school also means you'll unlikely be able to transfer your credits, apply for a Master of Fine Arts degree, or even gain employment at companies that require a bachelor's degree.

4. Academics

Academics at fine arts schools fall heavily into the category of building practical skills, often referred to by colleges as "applied training." While you will no doubt learn plenty about the history and philosophy of your art while earning your BFA, what you're really looking for is a curriculum

Remember: you may have additional expenses above and beyond what students at traditional colleges may pay. Art supplies each year can easily run into the thousands of dollars.

Students at fine arts colleges sometimes tend to deemphasize academics in favor of applied training, so some colleges are creating required curricula designed for first-year students. For example, all students at the Otis College of Art + Design enroll in the "Foundation Program," which teaches critical thinking and other core skills.

that can help you build a body of work. Besides, with all your free money tied up in art supplies, you probably can't afford to buy $500 worth of textbooks each semester anyway.

If you're pursuing a bachelor's degree, don't put the right side of your brain in storage just yet: you'll likely have to take a variety of classes. At the North Carolina School of the Arts, degree candidates must take coursework in the humanities, the social/behavioral sciences, and mathematics/natural sciences. The best academic programs will teach you how these different disciplines relate to your artwork so that it doesn't seem like you're just going through the motions of earning a degree.

Good fine arts schools will also supplement a solid academic program with the resources you need to be a better student. One of the factors that may influence your decision, for example, are a college's facilities, or lack thereof. Make sure you ask college representatives if first-year students have the same access to studio space or equipment as upperclassmen. Some colleges keep their facilities open 24 hours a day, 7 days a week, which you might appreciate the next time your muse wakes you at 2:00 A.M.

5. Campus Life

The good news about many fine arts schools is that you won't necessarily have to give up the traditional college campus scene. While intercollegiate athletics are reserved for those schools that are part of a larger college or university, sole-purpose fine arts colleges have an abundance of student clubs and organizations. Not surprisingly, many of these tend to be related to the finer things in life. Here are just a few examples:

- Animation club at the Minneapolis College of Art and Design

- Film society at the California College of the Arts
- Jazz band at the Manhattan School of Music

Traditional clubs exist as well. The Art Institute of Boston has a chapter of Amnesty International as well as a student newspaper. Ringling School of Art and Design in Sarasota, Florida, has a fraternity and a sorority for those who want to go Greek. And the University of the Arts in Philadelphia even has a fencing club.

As a burgeoning artist, you may be most interested in using the campus to showcase your work. Many fine arts schools fund campus exhibits and festivals that promote student work. Other good art schools add a bit of excitement to campus life by sponsoring visiting artists to either serve as instructors or share their experiences with students. When looking for the right school, ask the admissions officer how the college helps its students deliver their work to the larger public.

6. Residential Life

Some, but not all, fine arts colleges offer vibrant residential life options. Juilliard requires first-year students to live on campus, and many traditional universities with fine arts colleges are even offering innovative residence life programs. Texas Tech University has created what it calls the "Fine Arts Learning Community," designed specifically for fine arts majors. This community offers students the ability to live and learn among other artists, as well as receive support and guidance from college staff and faculty.

Resident life at many fine arts colleges gives you the opportunity to interact fully with artists in different disciplines. Some colleges specifically pair musicians and painters in the same dorm room so that each can gain an appreciation for the other. Plus, living with another tor-

Campus life, if a bit smaller (and a lot more stylish), is alive and well at fine arts schools across the country.

Juilliard students live in Lincoln Center in the heart of New York City, on one of the top twelve floors of the Rose Building.

tured artist may give you an idea of what your parents may have had to put up with for the last eighteen years.

7. Atmosphere

Whether public or private college, large or small, what characterizes the best fine arts schools is a sense of community. Students at these schools are often much more concerned about developing their skills alongside fellow artists than in grades or degrees. For this reason, the college visit is as important as any research when trying to select the right fit.

The atmosphere at a fine arts college sometimes takes on a life of its own, attracting the outside community. The atmosphere at the Mason Gross School of the Arts, part of Rutgers University, inextricably links education and art, to the point that nearly every night of the week is filled with performances, exhibitions, music, and dance. The campus brings together both students and outside artists and attracts a public eager to buy tickets for a glimpse. Summerfest, once a monthlong collection of exhibits and performances, has now grown into a year-round series.

Location is a factor that defines the atmosphere of many fine arts colleges. Not surprisingly, the most well-known fine arts schools are located in urban areas, often in close proximity to or even in partnership with the nation's great museums. Well-known fine arts programs call many big cities home, including:

- Seattle
- Los Angeles
- San Francisco
- Chicago
- New York
- Boston
- Philadelphia

Your choice of school may come down to which city provides the right atmosphere for creating your future works of art.

8. Students

Perhaps the best way of finding out about fine arts college students is by visiting a school's website, many of which now highlight current and past student accomplishments. The Cleveland Institute of Art, for example, uses its website to allow students to write about their experiences. The University of the Arts gives students web space to display samples of their work, including short films. The North Carolina School of the Arts includes a lengthy site detailing famous student alumni (admit it—you always wondered where Mary-Louise Parker and Jada Pinkett-Smith honed those acting skills).

Even though the fine arts industry can be cutthroat, fine arts students often check that competitiveness at the classroom door. Part of this is because students focus much less on their grades than students at other colleges, where grades play a more direct role in job prospects. But fine arts school students are definitely not slackers. The Maine College of Art recently announced several prestigious awards for its students, including a Guggenheim Fellowship and a Provincetown Fine Arts Work Center Fellowship.

9. Professors

When looking for good professors at a prospective fine arts school, you might want to be more concerned about the professional contributions faculty have made to the field rather than how many have earned a Ph.D. For this reason, fine arts colleges typically have fewer faculty members with advanced degrees than traditional universities—though they may still be among the brightest teachers in the land. Many have a long history of success in helping young artists become superstars, and they also win their fair share of prestigious academic awards, including Fulbright Awards and Guggenheim Fellowships.

The fine arts colleges also have an almost unique ability of attracting successful artists from the real world. The Massachusetts College of Art is a great example of a college that brings in outside artists year-round to lead lectures, interact with students, and display their work. When selecting a college, try and find out which of your top choices have been able to bring in the artists that you interest you. As long as you're paying tuition, you might as well learn from those who have been successful.

FAMOUS
Art School Alumni

1

Miles Davis: Juilliard School

2

Marcia Cross: Juilliard School

3

Chris Parnell: North Carolina School of the Arts

4

Quincy Jones: Berklee College of Music

5

Gus Van Sant: Rhode Island School of Design

6

Brendan Fraser: Cornish College of the Arts

7

David Sedaris: Art Institute of Chicago

8

Don Cheadle: California Institute of the Arts

9

Donna Karan: Parsons School of Design

10

Marc Jacobs: Parsons School of Design

10. The Intangibles

The fine arts campus may be your first introduction to a community of artists. This community can be intimidating, especially if you come from a high school with a small or barely existing art program. Fortunately, you can choose from a tremendous variety of fine arts colleges, ranging from thousands of students within large universities to just a few hundred students at small art schools focused entirely on one discipline.

You need to know about graduation rates at fine and performing arts colleges nationally. There is an unfortunate trend among students at these schools of dropping out before earning a degree—these schools have some of the lowest retention rates among all colleges.

Even the most prestigious fine and performing arts colleges suffer from this trend. Less than half of all Berklee College of Music students earn their degree, in part because so many dropouts, including John Mayer, Melissa Etheridge, and Gavin DeGraw, have gone on to stardom. Many students think that completing a degree is actually a hindrance to a successful career in the fine arts and purposefully withdraw before graduation. Just remember that for every superstar there are countless waiters and waitresses paying off student loans, still waiting to make it big.

Is This the Right Choice?

If you've determined that your life's calling is one of the fine arts, then there's little question about choosing a fine arts school. But remember that you have more choices than you probably think, including both public and private colleges. The North Carolina School of Arts and the Massachusetts College of Art are both public colleges that focus exclusively on the arts. Other public institutions, such as the University of Florida, have their own fine arts colleges, as well. These can be great choices for students who want to study art but also enjoy the benefits that come with being part of a larger community of students.

If you want to surround yourself with other students who share a very specific interest and where the curriculum concentrates exclusively or almost exclusively on the fine arts, then a fine arts school could be the choice for you. Just remember that picking the right fine arts school might not only make you a better artist but also keep you from wasting several thousand dollars in tuition and fees.

TWO-YEAR SCHOOLS

"With enormous classes and graduate teaching assistants, a big university seemed like a waste of money—especially when I could earn the first two years of my degree at a community college. I'm taking four classes this fall, all with fewer than twenty-five students. I can't imagine trying to learn any other way."

Mary
Rio Hondo Community College

CLUES
They Might *Not* Be for You

1

You're primarily interested in a four-year degree at a
highly selective university.

2

You're desperate to spend all of your college savings as
quickly as possible.

3

You don't believe it's possible to get a quality education in two years.

4

You rank *practical* near the bottom of your personal attributes.

5

You want to be in the pond for as long as possible.

6

You prefer your instructor to teach from theory rather than practice.

7

Being on a first-name basis with your teacher just doesn't seem right.

8

You're planning on being in college—and out of the workforce—
for as long as possible.

9

You suffer from tachophobia (a fear of speed).

10

Word association: someone says "technical," you say "difficulties."

Got two years? Then you can get a degree at a two-year school. Community colleges, or junior colleges, primarily offer two-year Associate of Arts (A.A.) and Associate of Applied Science (A.A.S) degrees in a wide variety of fields, and at many of these colleges you can pretty much study anything that you would at a four-year college or university. Many community colleges also have extensive student activities programs and intercollegiate athletic programs, with many athletes eventually going on to star at major NCAA programs during their junior and senior years.

Technical colleges, which also offer two-year programs, focus primarily on providing students with a specific skill, primarily offering Associate of Technical Arts (A.T.A.) and Associate of Applied Science (A.A.S.) degrees. These colleges offer a diverse range of programs, anything from degrees in automotive repair to web development. In general, technical colleges specialize in training students for entering the workforce, as opposed to preparing them to pursue a four-year degree.

At a Glance

Ten million students in America attend community and technical colleges, for a variety of reasons. Some students just have no interest in living in a dorm, attending a bowl game, or joining a club. Some students don't want to pay a small fortune for their degree, so, to save money, they attend a community college with the intention of eventually transferring to a four-year school. Understanding the following 10 things about two-year schools may help you decide if this is the right choice for you.

1. Selectivity

Two-year colleges admit the majority of applicants, so getting in shouldn't be a problem. You'll typically need only your high school diploma or GED—and you likely won't have to take the ACT or SAT. Instead, community and technical colleges generally administer assessment tests, which do not determine admission but the level of classes you can start taking. Two-year colleges often serve as great "second chance" schools for below-average high school students.

LARGEST
Community Colleges

1

Miami-Dade CC: 57,026

2

Houston CC: 39,838

3

Northern Virginia CC: 39,353

4

Southern Nevada CC: 34,204

5

Pima CC (Arizona): 31,216

6

College of DuPage (Illinois): 29,854

7

City College of San Francisco: 33,425

8

Valencia CC (Florida): 29,447

9

Santa Monica CC (California): 24,497

10

Austin CC (Texas): 35,576

Many of those same students whose high school grades kept them out of the four-year college of their first choice are eventually able to earn stellar grades at a two-year school. With their shiny new academic record, they manage to become very competitive transfer students. If you think your high school grades are too low to gain admission or scholarships at a four-year school, a two-year college strategy might be just the approach you need.

2. Reputation

The two-year schools rarely receive any national attention from the college ranking systems. Reputation among these schools is strictly a local affair, which makes sense, since most two-year colleges are rooted firmly in nearby communities. But some two-year colleges are well known among admissions counselors at four-year colleges for producing quality transfer students in a variety of academic disciplines. These schools include:

- Sinclair Community College in Ohio
- Valencia Community College in Florida
- Lane Community College in Oregon

Two-year colleges also vary in reputation by discipline. Most of the nation's first-responders, nurses, firefighters, and police officers receive their training at community and technical colleges, so you might actually advance your career by choosing one of these schools for your training. Some two-year colleges, such as Clover Park Technical College in Washington and Northwest Arkansas Community College, also train many of the nation's best computer security experts, who often earn more money with their associate's degrees than many students with bachelor's degrees.

3. Cost

When it comes to cost, no school can match the two-year schools for value. Want to earn a four-year degree in Kansas? You can study for the entire four years at the University of Kansas for $139 per credit hour or take your first two years at Hutchinson Community College for only $49 per credit hour. That's a tuition savings of over $4,300 for the very same bachelor's degree.

But lower tuition doesn't tell the whole story. University costs usually include a variety of additional fees, from health services to student union charges, which add to your bill—and which community and technical colleges often don't tack on. Other expenses, such as parking, books, and supplies, usually add up much more quickly at four-year colleges, making two-year schools even more of a bargain. Plus, many community and technical college students live at home, since the vast majority of people live within driving distance of at least one two-year college.

Be aware, though, that community and technical colleges typically have much less financial aid available than four-year schools. Some two-year schools offer only Pell Grants and state grants to their students. Generally, though, if cost is your driving factor in choosing a college, you can hardly go wrong with the two-year college system.

4. Academics

Community and technical colleges are primarily concerned with teaching students specific knowledge and skills. Unlike the liberal arts colleges, the two-year schools rely more heavily on multiple-choice tests, as well as memorizing material. Some recently graduated high school students find this a good match, since the teaching methods are similar to what they encountered in high school.

Many private two-year colleges have popped up over the past few years, and not all them are accredited, which means you won't be able to receive federal student aid—and might even be victim of a scam. Take caution when thinking about enrolling at an unaccredited college of any kind.

Among the vocational fields taught by community and technical colleges, academics seem much more like job skills training, with students learning their profession by actually doing the work. Students in these programs are often highly successful at finding employment right after graduating because they have real-life experience in their fields, either through internships, part-time jobs, or practicum assignments. If you want to gain usable skills in a highly specialized vocational field, a two-year school is your best choice.

5. Campus Life

Life does exist on two-year campuses, but it's not quite the same as at their four-year counterparts. Since students attend for only two years, they tend to invest less time in creating and building student clubs and organizations. Student-activities budgets at two-year colleges usually pale in comparison to those of the four-year schools, so students have fewer resources and facilities. But this lack of interest and funding can work to your advantage: if one of your college goals is to be student body president or the president of a student organization, you may find the path a little easier at a two-year school, where there is less competition.

Two-year colleges even offer competitive sports programs, and many of today's best athletes actually got their start in the junior college system. If you're a prospective athlete, you may want to attend a two-year college just to keep your own athletic dreams alive. You'll have a much easier time making the team of a junior college than you would at a four-year university.

The nation's community and technical colleges train 65 percent of America's healthcare workers.

KINDS OF
Community College Degrees

1
Associate of Arts

2
Associate of Applied Arts

3
Associate of Applied Science

4
Associate of General Studies

5
Associate in Nursing

6
Associate in Occupational Studies

7
Associate in Science

8
Associate in Specialized Business

9
Associate in Technical Studies

10
Associate in Technology

6. Residential Life

Most students attend a two-year school that's close to home, so living on campus usually ranks pretty low on their college wish list. For this reason, only a small handful of two-year colleges offer dormitories for their students. Even fewer colleges offer the wide range of support services typically associated with residential universities, so living on campus at a two-year college is not all that different from simply renting an apartment, albeit one very close to campus.

If the two-year college you pick does offer residence halls, you should definitely consider taking advantage. Dorm life will help you build a sense of community with your fellow students and give you easier access to classes and facilities. Many students opt out of residential life because it's cheaper to live at home, but they probably don't realize that students who live at home will likely receive less financial aid. Student financial aid offices base your financial aid eligibility, or "cost of attendance," on many factors, one of which is whether you live at home. Students who live at home have a lower cost of attendance because they presumably don't have to pay rent or utilities.

If you do choose to live on campus, time is of the essence. Central Oregon Community College, for example, can only offer dorm rooms to about 100 of its 1,600 full-time students. The two-year college you choose may have even fewer opportunities, so act fast.

7. Atmosphere

Although two-year schools enroll a fair number of students, the casual onlooker might describe the community college atmosphere as somewhat less than exciting. Such is the nature of the two-year college system. Many

Curt Schilling, the all-star pitcher who helped the Red Sox end "the curse" in 2004, got his start at Yavapai Community College in Arizona.

students at these schools live off-campus, hold part-time or even full-time jobs, and often have families of their own. They don't necessarily have a lot of time for mingling with other students at the student union.

Community and technical college campuses also reflect their workforce training missions, as a great deal of learning takes place off campus. Nursing students often earn many of their college credits in area hospitals. Aviation students will likely be found at a local airport. Paramedicine students may be spending most of their time responding to real calls in the back of an ambulance. Technical colleges, in particular, focus on specialization, and their atmospheres reflect this by being more compartmentalized than four-year colleges, where students often spend their entire first two years undecided in a major.

8. Students

In general, there are two types of students at two-year colleges:

- Transfer students
- Vocational students

Transfer students eventually plan on attending a four-year college and earning their bachelor's degree. These students often choose the two-year college route because of cost, location, convenience, and/or more favorable admissions requirements. They focus primarily on general education courses to earn an associate of arts degree that will be accepted by a four-year college. The one advantage these students have over first-years and sophomores at four-year colleges is that at the end of their two years, they have an actual academic degree that they can include as one more line on their résumés.

The second type of student is the vocational student. These individuals want to receive very specialized training and education that will allow them to immediately enter the workforce. In most cases, these students take all their classes together, and though they may not have a lot of interaction with the rest of the student body, as a small group they can become quite close-knit.

In both cases, most students at two-year colleges are what the National Center for Education Statistics defines as "nontraditional." A nontraditional student is anyone who:

In 2002, almost 90 percent of two-year college students were considered nontraditional.

- Has not entered college immediately after high school
- Attends classes part-time
- Works thirty-five hours per week
- Is considered financially independent of his or her parents
- Is a parent
- Has earned a GED

Often, students at two-year colleges are older than twenty-four years of age, and the student body is much better represented by ethnic minorities, further adding to the general diversity of the campus.

9. Professors

Like students, two-year college professors are a mix of two general categories:

Nationally, only around 20 percent of two-year college instructors have an earned doctorate or advanced professional degree.

- Instructors who focus on academic courses
- Instructors of specialized trades and vocations

Those of the first type teach many of the same subjects you might find at a four-year school, such as math or history. These professors went to school themselves to become teachers and often choose to work in the two-year college system, which focuses much more on undergraduate instruction and much less on faculty research.

Those of the second type generally come directly from industry and are recruited by community and technical colleges to pass their real-life knowledge on to students. These instructors may not have necessarily gone to col-

10

NOTABLE

Alumni of Community and Technical Colleges

1

Jerry Crutchfield, President, MCA Publishing

2

Gwendolyn Brooks, poet

3

Rita Mae Brown, author/activist

4

Kweisi Mfume, former President/CEO, NAACP

5

Allen Boyd, Florida congressman

6

James Belushi, actor

7

Nolan Ryan, Hall of Fame pitcher

8

Francis Scobee, NASA astronaut

9

Lloyd Hackley, past President, North Carolina
Community College System

10

Eduardo Padron, President, Miami Dade College

lege to become teachers, but their in-depth and firsthand knowledge helps them give their students a leg up when it comes time to look for a job.

Two-year college professors are often much more engaged with their students and tend to lecture to their students much less than you might find in your typical freshman-level class at a university. Also, even though your professor may not go by the title of Doctor, you can rest assured that your class will not be led by a graduate student teaching assistant. And you can also be much more confident that your professor can back up his or her words with real-life experience.

10. The Intangibles

While both community and technical college degrees can be transferred to four-year colleges and universities, there are some caveats. If you intend on pursuing a degree at one of the highly competitive elite colleges, you may find it practically impossible to gain entry as a student transferring from a two-year college. Even some less selective universities may not completely accept all of your college credits even if you do gain admission.

If you intend to transfer to a four-year school, look for community and technical colleges with articulation agreements. Articulation agreements are contracts between two- and four-year schools that specify which degrees and credits will transfer when you pursue your bachelor's degree. The best articulation agreements allow students to transfer all of their credits. Otherwise, you may sacrifice any cost savings you hoped to gain by attending a two-year school.

When it comes to job placement, be very direct when asking questions of the college's admissions representatives. As mentioned, technical colleges primarily train

Transfer considerations and job placement are the bread and butter of the two-year system, and the best community and technical colleges will be able to answer any questions you may have about them.

TWO-YEAR COLLEGES
That Offer a Bachelor's Degree

A growing trend among two-year schools is to offer certain four-year degrees.

1

Chipola College (Florida)

2

Great Basin College (Nevada)

3

Miami-Dade College

4

St. Petersburg College (Florida)

5

Morrisville State College (New York)

6

Dixie State College (Utah)

7

SUNY College of Technology at Alfred (New York)

8

Westark Community College (Arkansas)

9

Honolulu Community College

10

South Texas College

students for entry into the workforce. Some careers, including high-paying fields in computer science and health, just don't require a bachelor's degree. However, in choosing the right technical college, you'll want to find one with a good record of job placement, particularly programs that place students directly into internships or apprenticeships while they earn their degrees.

Is This the Right Choice?

Even if you eventually hope to earn a four-year degree, a two-year college might be the right school to get you started. Two-year colleges have many benefits that you might be aware of, such as lower costs, and a few benefits you might not have considered, such as quality of teaching. Of course, you'll also be postponing the big-college experience, which ultimately may not be worth the savings in tuition.

However, if you do choose to start your academic career at a community or technical college, one thing you won't have to worry about is a lack of educational quality. With small class sizes, diverse student bodies, professors with real-life experience in their fields, and a price you can afford, it's a wonder that more students don't make the two-year choice.

7 CAREER SCHOOLS

"In high school, I studied auto restoration and knew that I wanted to be a motorcycle mechanic. Going to a regular college just seemed like a waste when the skills I needed were offered by the local trade school."

Brian
Universal Technical Institute

CLUES
They Might *Not* Be for You

1

You'd rather do all your learning inside a classroom.

2

You prefer teachers whose last names end in Ph.D.

3

You don't believe it's possible to get training for a job in fewer than two
years.

4

You rank *hand-eye coordination* near the bottom of your
personal attributes.

5

You want to be a fish in a well-respected pond.

6

You want to pursue a career that requires an advanced degree.

7

None of your outfits go particularly well with a blue collar.

8

You're planning on paying for your entire education with need-based
federal financial aid.

9

You suffer from ergophobia (a fear of work).

10

Word association: someone says "career," you say "counseling."

Private career schools include for-profit institutions where students enroll to learn a practical skill that is required for entry into the workforce. The private career schools broadly encompass what are known as for-profit proprietary schools and traditional trade schools. For-profit proprietary schools tend to have a broader scope, offering many different types of degree programs, whereas traditional trade schools usually focus on one specific field, such as barbering. Proprietary schools tend to follow workforce trends and quickly put together educational programs to match, with current hot topics including biotechnology and e-commerce. The largest of these schools have over one hundred "campuses" in cities across the country, though these campuses might be better described as offices or classrooms.

Trade schools tend to focus on one specific field and offer training that tends to be hands-on. Some good examples include schools of culinary arts, flight schools, and cosmetology schools. These schools often offer certificates instead of degrees. But be aware that each state has very specific licensure requirements for members of certain trades, such as plumbers or electricians. If you feel a trade school is right for you, you should contact the appropriate state licensing agency to make sure the school you choose offers a legitimate education.

At a Glance

Private career schools share few similarities with the other colleges listed in this guide. They offer one thing and one thing only: specialized training for entry into the workforce or career advancement. For-profit schools, in particular, have seen tremendous growth in the number of enrolled students over the past ten years by responding directly to market demands. But they also operate on a business model, meaning you'll have to be very careful when speaking with their so-called admissions counselors, who are more likely to be trained in sales than education. Knowing all you can about these schools will be important when deciding if this is the right choice for you.

10

Proprietary Schools

With the exception of Missouri Tech, these schools have campuses all over the country. You can find the locations nearest to you by visiting the schools' websites.

1

DeVry University

2

Corinthian Colleges

3

Strayer University

4

ITT Technical Institute

5

Gibbs College

6

ECPI College of Technology

7

National College of Business and Technology

8

Missouri Tech

9

Herzing College

10

Bryant and Stratton College

1. Selectivity

Career schools can't be beat when it comes to universal selectivity. If you can pay the tuition, you can receive the training. Most private career schools accept virtually every student and have even been accused of being too lenient in their admission practices. The Business Career Training Institute (BCTI), with campuses in Washington and Oregon, has even been sued for taking tuition dollars from individuals who are unable to complete their training. BCTI has since suspended its operations.

The downside to universal selectivity is that there is no way to guarantee that your fellow students will contribute to your learning. Plus, employers may not value your degree, especially if you can receive the same training at a more competitive and fully accredited community or technical college. On the other hand, if your academic record makes it impossible to gain admission at a regular college, a private career school might be your only option.

Two-year, for-profit schools have grown far more rapidly than any other kind of two-year school and now make up around 30 percent of the market.

2. Reputation

Private career colleges, when compared with other kinds of schools, generally fall at the very bottom of the reputation charts, for several reasons:

- Most are not accredited by higher education agencies.
- Several have recently gone out of business.
- Many will admit just about every student, regardless of ability.
- As for-profit schools, they often have a business focus, and their employees, including the instructors, usually don't have a background in education.

Local employers, however, may have favorable opinions of some of these schools, especially the ones that train work-

10

High-Wage, High-Demand Trades

The U.S. Department of Labor has released projections that the
following fields will produce high-wage, high-demand jobs:

1

Advanced manufacturing

2

Automotive services

3

Biotechnology

4

Construction

5

Geospatial technology

6

Health services

7

Hospitality

8

Information technology

9

Retail trade

10

Transportation

ers in fields not addressed by regular colleges and universities. And some private career colleges do have solid reputations. The Culinary Institute of America in New York, for example, is well known for producing quality chefs. It is also fully accredited, grants associate's and bachelor's degrees, and offers financial aid, including merit-based scholarships.

Students choose career schools when they are certain about the industry in which they'd like to work. If this describes you, then one way to make the right college choice is to speak directly with current professionals, rather than current students. For example, if you want to be an aviation mechanic, one thing you can do is to contact the human resources office of someone who hires in this field, such as Boeing or McDonnell Douglas. They can probably give you an idea of which schools they feel have the best reputation based on any graduates they may have hired in the past.

3. Cost

If you choose a private career college, you have a lot of cost considerations to think about. Some of these schools charge as much or more than even the Ivy League colleges, when you consider the cost per credit hour. And many of the most expensive of these schools do not have accreditation, which the Department of Education requires for its student financial aid programs. This means that you will likely have to borrow through private loan programs to pay tuition and fees. Private loans often charge much higher interest rates than federal loans and do not grant you any grace period for repayment.

Some of the more well-known colleges, such as DeVry University, do participate in federal financial aid programs, including Pell Grants and work-study. But even some that are approved to participate in federal programs

The National Center for Educational Statistics shows that students at two-year, for-profit colleges graduate sooner and earn higher initial salaries than students at public community colleges.

10

Specialized Career Programs

1

Aromatherapy

2

Barbering

3

Cosmetology/Esthetics

4

Diving

5

Floral design

6

Culinary arts

7

Gardening/Landscaping

8

Mapping/Surveying

9

Personal fitness

10

Photography

aren't always eligible for state financial aid, such as state grants, work-study, and state student loans. If the college isn't eligible for state aid, you might be better off seeing if a different school, such as a public community or technical college, offers the same programs.

A full list of state higher education agencies can be found at the end of this book.

The other important thing to consider is the school's financial well-being. Several for-profit colleges have gone bankrupt in recent years, leaving their former students without a degree or certificate and with heavy student loan debts. The school itself is highly unlikely to admit its financial troubles to a prospective student, so your best course of action is to contact your state's higher education agency. Most state higher education agencies investigate claims of fraud among local colleges, so if any violations have occurred they can likely inform you of the details.

4. Academics

The career colleges represent the ultimate in "learning by doing," as opposed to learning by reading. The tests consist mainly of practical exams, and success in these colleges will be determined by how well you can physically perform the tasks related to your career.

For-profit colleges do not want to see students fail, and, for better or worse, few students ever do.

While career colleges may not always offer paper examinations, you shouldn't throw away your number 2 pencil. While your certificate may be useful, it may not allow you to perform your trade in the state where you reside. States usually have their own licensure examinations for many trades. Some professions, such as Emergency Medical Technicians, even have national examinations. Before you enroll in a career school, find out in writing how well graduates typically do on licensure examinations. Your certificate or degree is only as good as your professional license.

A career school might be the right choice for you if you want to get specific job-skills training, but it isn't the best option if you want to start a long academic career. You'll likely find it difficult, if not impossible, to get credit for your career college degree or certificate at another school, since most traditional colleges don't hold for-profit career colleges in high esteem.

5. Campus Life

Students choose career colleges exclusively for professional training, so campus life at these schools is virtually nonexistent. Don't expect to participate in student clubs, root for the home football team, or even access services from a student counseling center or library: for-profit schools don't offer any of these. Students at these colleges rarely ask for them, and these kinds of services are usually very expensive. Harvard, for instance, spends roughly $50 million each year to maintain its library. Private career colleges could never maintain this level of campus life and continue to make a profit.

If some semblance of campus life is important to you, you'll probably be better off choosing a community college that offers the same professional training. On the other hand, if your only goal is to receive job training, the shortest distance between your two points might very well have a career college at one end and a job at the other.

6. Residential Life

With the absence of campus life, you might be surprised to find out that some career schools do offer housing—but you won't find a comprehensive residential life program that offers academic and social support for students, as you would at a nonprofit institution of higher education. The purpose of housing at for-profit schools is to keep all students together to complete their training as quickly as possible—and to make additional profit. Make sure that you understand the fees involved before signing on the dotted line.

Many trade programs last fifteen weeks or fewer, so any available housing is temporary. You may even find out that your "dormitory" is actually a shared room at a private motel. For this reason, you need to consider the fact that while you are paying to live "on campus," you may also need to keep up to date with your rent payments at your permanent residence—essentially doubling your housing costs while in school.

7. Atmosphere

Ivy-covered walls, redbrick-lined walkways, the excitement of students returning to campus among falling leaves, and cool, crisp breezes certainly do not describe the atmosphere at the typical career college. Instead, you'll probably find yourself in an actual working environment to complete your training. For example:

- Culinary arts students work in kitchens
- Emergency medical technician students work in the backs of ambulances
- Cosmetology students work in actual salons

This kind of real-life atmosphere can be very attractive to students who learn with their hands.

Some career schools that focus in areas such as business and computer applications do offer training in more "traditional" classrooms, often offices leased in commercial areas or shopping centers. You might not feel the satisfying crunch of fallen leaves underneath your footsteps as you cross the campus commons, but there's usually plenty of free parking to make up for it.

8. Students

For-profit career colleges cater to the working adult, so your classmates will probably be nontraditional. In other words, most will be older than twenty-four years of age, working either full- or part-time, and/or supporting a family of their own. Some may already have college degrees and choose a career college to build concrete skills for advancement within their current

Red Flags

Not every for-profit school has your best interests in mind.
Look out for recruiters who:

1

Are overly pushy

2

Make threats

3

Ask for cash deposits

4

Pressure you to sign application forms

5

Guarantee financial assistance

6

Avoid answering questions about the
college's accreditation or financial status

7

Have only PO boxes

8

Will not give you the names of their direct supervisors

9

Work out of their homes

10

Appear unkempt or unprofessional

organizations. Some may have recently been laid off or discharged from the military and are looking for a career change. A few may not have the academic credentials necessary to enter a more traditional college.

Students at career colleges will have at least one thing in common: they've chosen to study a highly specialized trade. Student groups, or cohorts, often begin and finish their training together and often go on to work or do business together upon graduation. This kind of close-knit learning can be one of the best aspects of studying at a for-profit career school.

"My dream growing up was to become a firefighter, pure and simple. Going to a four-year college would have been a big mistake for me."

Andrew
Firefighter

9. Professors

Even more so than community and technical college instructors, career college professors come directly from industry. They teach from their own work experience, and their methods of instruction reflect this. Not only can they teach you the tools of the trade, but they can also share the behind-the-scenes secrets of their professions. This can definitely give students at career colleges an advantage over students who learn only from books or theory.

Career college instructors often have direct ties to private industry, so when students begin their job hunt, their instructors are sometimes able to assist them with recommendations or referrals. As the saying goes, it's not always what you know, but whom you know, that really counts.

10. The Intangibles

You might say that the characteristics of private career schools mimic the characteristics of the professions for which they are meant to train. If you study at an automotive school, such as Westwood College in Colorado, you'll actually spend your days in a real, working shop. If you enroll at an underwater diving school, such as the Commercial

Diving Academy in Jacksonville, Florida, your "classroom" will be the waters of the St. Johns River. Career schools train from real-life practice, as opposed to theory. If you desire hands-on training, one of these schools might be the right choice.

Time is of the essence when it comes to career schools. For-profit schools, especially trade schools, understand that the quicker they can get you trained, the sooner they can enroll new students. Many students complete their training in fifteen weeks or fewer and, depending on state licensing requirements, enter the workforce soon after. Students don't take any sort of general education courses or degree prerequisites. Career schools teach only those courses that they consider essential to your career.

If you know you want to pursue a trade, a career school might be just the thing. But you'll have to exercise more precaution in selecting a private career college than you would with any nonprofit institution of higher education, since these schools don't undergo the same rigid accreditation process as public community and technical colleges. As with any for-profit venture, you'll need to take a buyer-beware approach to picking the right school.

Is This the Right Choice?

As institutions focused on teaching a specific workforce-related skill, these schools seem much like community and technical colleges. They don't offer much, if anything, in the way of student activities, residence halls, or athletics. Class sizes are usually quite small, even smaller than those at liberal arts colleges. As private, for-profit schools, however, tuition usually runs much higher than community and technical colleges, and most of these institutions do not offer federal financial aid such as Pell Grants or Stafford loans. You will also find it more difficult to transfer your credits to another school if you decide you want to earn a bachelor's degree elsewhere.

However, if you've decided that you want to go directly into the workforce, have located a trade that is taught only by a for-profit career school, or have been turned away from other institutions of higher education due to grades, then these schools might be right for you.

DISTANCE-LEARNING SCHOOLS

"I wanted to go to college—but I had a family and a full-time job, which made taking classes at a traditional campus difficult. With some hard work and good time-management skills, I earned a degree from my own home. Distance learning was the perfect solution."

Helene
Western Governors University

CLUES
They Might *Not* Be for You

1

You require face-to-face instruction.

2

You consider sitting in a balcony in a 300-student lecture hall to be the most distance you can handle.

3

You've spent the last eighteen years trying to get OUT of your house.

4

You rank *self-motivation* near the bottom of your list of personal attributes.

5

You don't care if you're in a big pond or a small pond— you just want to be in the pond.

6

You can't imagine college without classroom discussion.

7

You've already purchased four years' worth of killer outfits.

8

Your New Year's resolutions included a six-month internet moratorium.

9

You suffer from oikophobia (a fear of home surroundings).

10

Word association: someone says "out of sight," you say "out of mind."

With major advances in home computer technology, many colleges have given students the option to earn either partial or entire bachelor's degrees without leaving their homes. Traditional colleges that have a physical campus are known as "brick and mortar" schools. Students at these schools can take classes on or off campus. "Online colleges" don't have a main campus and offer all of their educational courses via distance learning. Most online colleges are private, for-profit institutions, though a few, such as Empire State College in New York, are public, not-for-profit schools.

Distance learning is not restricted to the internet. Some brick and mortar schools have set up satellite rooms in offices away from their main campus for students too far away to drive to class. These colleges use live video links that allow students to interact in real time with fellow students and teachers. Other colleges rely on pretaped lessons, either broadcast via television or distributed as VHS tapes or DVDs. Even online-only colleges have gotten into the act. The University of Phoenix, for example, one of the largest online colleges, has 163 "learning centers" across the country for distance learners who are looking for face time with fellow students and instructors.

If you investigate this option, you'll find that many terms are used to describe distance education:

- Distance learning
- Distributed learning
- E-learning
- Web-based instruction
- Blended learning

- Cyber college
- Virtual college
- Asynchronous learning
- Internet college
- Computer-based training

At a Glance

Whether you want to earn an entire degree or just a few credits, you need to know all the pros and cons of distance learning. The ability to adapt a curriculum to meet your schedule and location may draw you to distance learning, and the fact that you won't have to worry about being up to date on the latest fashion doesn't hurt, either. But distance learning does take

GREAT

Distance-Learning Schools

1

Empire State College Center for Distance Learning
(State University of New York)

2

Fort Hays State University Virtual College (Kansas)

3

University of Maryland University College

4

DePaul University School for New Learning (Illinois)

5

School of New Resources, College of New Rochelle (New York)

6

Marylhurst University (Oregon)

7

University of Illinois Online

8

University of Massachusetts Online

9

University of Central Florida

10

Western Governors University (Utah)

discipline. The following 10 basics will give you a better idea if this is the right choice for you.

1. Selectivity

Selectivity varies among distance-learning programs, but most online colleges admit the majority of applicants. Because distance learning is relatively new, the competition may be less intense. However, some of the most elite colleges offer distance-learning options in one shape or another. Even Harvard University offers online courses through its Extension School (**www.extension.harvard. edu**).

Online colleges are usually private, for-profit institutions, and not all are accredited. If you are considering an online-only college, you need to spend more time researching both its accreditation and whether other colleges or employers will recognize the credits you earn. In a desire to take a shortcut to learning, some students have been burned by online schemes.

2. Reputation

The reputation of a distance-learning program at a college depends a great deal on whether the college is accredited. Accreditation agencies consist of regional or professional oversight bodies that determine whether a school meets high standards of education. If a school has not been accredited, you probably won't be able to transfer the credits you earn. Employers and graduate schools probably won't accept your degree as valid.

The most reputable distance-learning programs are those offered by traditionally accredited brick and mortar schools, particularly the state universities and the elite colleges. Most of these schools will clearly state that an online degree earned from their institutions is no different from a degree earned on campus. In other words,

In 2004, the University of Maryland University College had 126,341 online course enrollments.

A full list of accredited schools and accreditation agencies may be found on the Department of Education website, **www.ed.gov**.

10

TRADITIONAL COLLEGES
With Distance-Learning Degrees

1

Fort Hays State University (Kansas)

2

Lehigh University (Pennsylvania)

3

DePaul University (Illinois)

4

Utica College (New York)

5

Western Michigan University

6

Washington State University

7

University of Colorado

8

Oregon State University

9

Indiana State University

10

University of Tennessee

employers and graduate schools won't know that you earned your credits via the internet or through some other distance-learning means.

A few of the larger online colleges receive regional accreditation, and their students qualify for federal student financial aid. Some of the more reputable of these schools have articulation agreements with traditional colleges so that you don't have to worry about credits not transferring. A few of the better known programs include:

- DeVry University
- Western Governors University
- Regis University
- Kaplan University
- University of Phoenix

You'll need to exercise caution in choosing a school without a traditional campus. Ask online college representatives to provide evidence of accreditation, eligibility for federal financial aid, and proof of articulation agreements with other schools. Better yet, make them provide you with examples of graduate schools or employers that have accepted their degrees. If you're thinking about graduate school, contact a few reputable programs and ask them directly if they'll honor a degree from the online college you're considering.

3. Cost

Costs for distance-learning education range from surprisingly affordable to unexpectedly expensive. Because distance-learning degrees come from nearly every kind of college, you may have much more of a challenge in comparing sticker prices—but, handled correctly, you can realize significant savings by earning your degree online. For example, state residents who attend an in-state school

The Curious Cat Who Could

In December 2004, the Pennsylvania Attorney General's office sued Trinity Southern University in Texas for issuing fraudulent degrees online. The lawsuit came after Trinity Southern issued an MBA to Colby Nolan—the district attorney's six-year-old cat.

Because of the high interest rate of private loans, you should always opt for a fully accredited school that is approved by the Department of Education to process federal financial aid.

will usually pay the same tuition rates as other residents and will avoid many of the miscellaneous expenses faced by on-campus students, such as gas, parking, and possibly even some student fees.

On the other hand, to take advantage of distance-learning courses, you'll probably need to purchase computer equipment and have access to the internet. And if the college you choose is not accredited, you'll have to pay all expenses out of pocket or borrow through a private loan program, which will almost certainly have a higher interest rate than any of the federal student loans.

Even if you locate an accredited school, you may find that scholarships will be much harder to come by at the online colleges than the brick and mortar schools. Most online colleges, being for-profit businesses, do not easily part with their money. If you have any aspirations of paying for your degree with scholarships, you'll almost certainly need to choose a brick and mortar school.

Expenses You'll Avoid with Distance Learning:

1. Parking
2. Gas
3. Certain on-campus fees, such as lab or recreation charges
4. On-campus housing and dining
5. The latest college fashion accessories

. . . You'll Face with Distance Learning:

6. Computer equipment
7. Internet connection
8. Word processing software
9. Office desk and furniture
10. Extra pair of pajamas

4. Academics

Students have far fewer academic choices with distance learning since some subject areas aren't well suited to the internet or live television feeds. You may find that the classes you take are limited to just a few fields, such as business administration or criminal justice. Before enrolling in a school based on a promise of earning "any degree you want," make sure you receive a full list of classes and degrees that are offered.

The nature of the coursework will also differ from traditional campus-based teaching. Distance-learning coursework relies heavily on reading comprehension, since students don't have the luxury of having live instructors to guide them through lectures. And while distance-learning students working at home can study the material at their own pace, they face constant distractions not found in the typical classroom. Whether it's a ringing phone, an attention-needy pet, or an enticing slice of daytime television, distance learners face their fair share of academic obstacles.

Many distance-learning educators recommend ways that students can maximize their ability to work well at home:

- Try to set up an environment that feels like a traditional classroom, such as setting up your computer equipment on a real desk in a quiet room.
- Sit in a chair, rather than lie on the bed or carpet.
- Establish strict rules for your study hours, minimizing any distractions or time spent on the telephone or in front of the television.
- Better yet: get an answering machine and Tivo, and concentrate on your academic goals.

10 Distractions You Won't Find in a Classroom

1. ESPN, *General Hospital*, and *Oprah*
2. Instant Messenger
3. Yahoo, Hotmail, AOL, and Gmail
4. Needy pets
5. Endless phone calls
6. Chatty family members

COMMON
Distance-Learning Fields

1

Business administration

2

Criminal justice

3

Communication

4

Early childhood education

5

Computers/IT/Web development

6

Nursing

7

Environmental science

8

Paralegal studies

9

Hotel/Hospitality management

10

Accounting

7. "Urgent" errands
8. Snacks to prepare and eat
9. Online shopping
10. *Sports Illustrated* and *US Weekly*

5. Campus Life

If you decide to enroll in an online college, then you should be prepared to give up college social activities altogether. Some students choose distance learning for exactly that reason, but others don't always give student life much thought when making their decision. They forget that campus life consists of more than just frat parties and football games. Career counseling, guest speakers, and student activities all serve to enrich your college years. Students at online colleges need to consider whether the convenience of distance learning really outweighs the benefits of being on campus.

By taking distance-learning courses through a brick and mortar school, many students take advantage of the best of both worlds. Distance learners at Clemson University, for example, can participate in all campus activities even while they earn their degrees off site. If you desire the convenience of distance learning but still crave the comforts of campus life, this might be the right option for you.

6. Residential Life

Online college students give up the idea of residential life entirely. Distance learning has opened up educational opportunities to more students than ever before, particularly nontraditional students with full-time jobs or those who are raising a family while earning a degree. The downside is that many students consider the relationships they develop while living on campus to be as important as their diplomas, and online learners may never experience this kind of camaraderie.

Brick and mortar schools, on the other hand, usually allow any enrolled student, including distance learners, to live on campus. Students who live on campus, however, need to take even more precautions when pursuing an online degree. The distractions of dorm life have seriously overburdened even the most dedicated of traditional students. If you decide to live on

10

STUDENT SERVICES
Available Online

Just because you're at a distance doesn't mean you have to give up on student services.

1
Writing lab (Rogue Community College – Oregon)

2
Tutoring (Mercy College – New York)

3
Academic advising (University of Oregon)

4
Career planning (University of Minnesota–Duluth)

5
Career placement (University of Pennsylvania)

6
Testing (University of Oregon)

7
Disability resources (Rio Salado College – Arizona)

8
General guidance (DeAnza College – California)

9
Library services (University of Hawaii at Manoa)

10
Financial aid counseling (Grossmont College – California)

campus but fully intend to take classes via distance learning, you should consider two things:

- See if the residence hall system has "quiet" halls or convenient computer labs where you can study far away from your bongo-drum-playing roommate.
- Begin by taking no more than one distance-learning class per semester until you establish that this option will work for you.

7. Atmosphere

So what exactly does distance learning look like? If you enroll in an online college, you will more than likely complete most of your studies over the internet, using software provided by the school. The more established online schools may even assign you an advisor to help you through the process, from buying textbooks to assisting you with financial aid. When you pick classes, you'll download the "lectures," read them, or, in some cases, watch them through streaming video. You'll then complete quizzes and tests online when you're ready. Lessons are asynchronous, meaning students do not have to participate in lessons at the same time.

Brick and mortar schools with physical campuses sometimes take a different approach to distance learning by offering synchronous lessons. Synchronous lessons take place at one scheduled time, usually via a live televised video feed, and students must participate together, often in a classroom that may be hundreds of miles away from the main campus. Even though the instructor is far away, these lessons can seem very much like regular college classes: while you sit at your desk, you watch an instructor give a lecture, in real time. The instructor can even see you, since there will likely be a video camera in your classroom.

You can visit **www. blackboard.com** to get a glimpse of the most common distance-learning software used by colleges today.

Synchronous
lessons are a
popular option
for remote, rural
towns, whose
residents want to
attend a regional
state college
without relocating.

You should try to sit in on a distance-learning class or walk through an online tutorial to get a feel for this form of education.

8. Students

Successful distance-learning students have several qualities in common:

- They have a healthy dose of self-discipline, combined with independence and motivation.
- They are highly organized and able to stick to a routine.
- Because distance learning appeals to individuals with outside commitments, such as family or full-time jobs, students are typically older.
- They don't worry too much about missing out on typical college social activities.
- They need to be highly self-reliant, particularly when it comes to nonacademic issues such as answering their own financial aid and career guidance questions.
- Since distance-learning degrees are not available in every discipline, students concentrate in certain kinds of fields, such as business administration.

There are plenty of students who won't find distance-learning schools to be a good match:

- Students who enjoy participating with others or who rely on teachers for guidance and motivation often struggle in a distance-learning environment.
- If you tend to procrastinate, distance learning might seem like a good choice, since it allows you to study and complete assignments at your own pace. But procrastinators rarely succeed in asynchronous distance learning since they tend to put off everything to the last minute, until all the work becomes too overwhelming to complete.

If you have recently graduated from high school, you may be easily sold on the convenience of distance learning without considering the consequences. Students not well suited to this style of learning may wind up simply throwing away their hard-earned money.

9. Professors

You will likely have a range of differing experiences with your distance-learning instructors. Just as some students are not well suited to the intricacies of off-campus learning, some teachers have difficulty adapting to this form of education. If you attend a brick and mortar college, your instructor may be brand new to distance-learning education, and this may result in lost time as he or she fumbles through learning the technology. Also, some teachers who are quite good at giving students feedback in person may not be so responsive when it comes to email, which is one of the main ways distance learners communicate with their instructors.

On the other hand, experienced distance-learning educators have become skilled at this method of instruction as the field has grown. And some students remark that they find written feedback of their work via email much more valuable than meeting in person. Plus, many of the instructors of online classes come directly from industry. So even though they may have outside careers, you can often be sure that they are teaching from real-life practice as opposed to theory.

10. The Intangibles

The big intangible concerning distance learning is transferability. Even though 85 percent of all colleges offer some kind of online education, be prepared for raised eyebrows when you inform prospective employers that you did not earn your degree at a traditional, campus-based school.

Especially among the online colleges, faculty members may be much less qualified to teach than is typically required at a traditional, campus-based school. Like you, your online instructors may also have outside commitments, meaning that you are not exactly their first priority.

Donald Trump has even gotten into the distance-learning act, recently launching Trump University (**www. trumpuniversity. com**).

Distance learning is rapidly growing, but it has not quite reached adulthood.

What this means for you is that you have a little extra homework to do. Choosing the right distance-learning college will require you to research its reputation, accreditation status, financial aid eligibility, and graduate success rate. You should also ask yourself some hard questions: are you choosing distance learning because it's well suited to your learning style, or are you choosing it because you feel it's your only educational option? If you're choosing distance learning as a last resort, you might find yourself in a virtual mess if the doors you want it to open instead remain shut.

If you're drawn to distance learning, you're definitely not alone: the options for participating in it are vast, and its popularity is rising. The schools that offer distance-learning education range from elite universities to internet start-ups focused primarily on profit-making. What all these schools advertise in common is the ability to educate students in a way that fits their needs and their schedules. Students have responded so well to the draw of distance learning that at least 2 million students took at least one online course during the 2002 academic year.

Is This the Right Choice?

Taking advantage of increasingly universal technology, schools across the country have begun to embrace distance-learning education as part of their overall curricula. Distance-learning degrees particularly suit the needs of those who may have difficulty traveling to a traditional campus, often due to work, family, or physical constraints.

If you don't have these limitations, however, you might want to consider the things that distance-learning degree programs can't offer, which include the kinds of life-changing experiences and friendships that come only with being on campus. And even if distance learning is right for your geographical restrictions, it might be a poor fit for your learning style.

Only after considering all these factors will you be able to decide if a distance-learning school is right for you.

9
OVERSEAS SCHOOLS

"Most of the students were Germans, of course, but the representatives of foreign lands were very numerous. They hailed from every corner of the globe, —for instruction is cheap in Heidelberg, and so is living, too."

Mark Twain
A Tramp Abroad

CLUES

They Might *Not* Be Right for You

1

You require English-only instruction.

2

You can't stand the way you look in your passport photo.

3

The thought of buying toiletries by making hand gestures sends you to your "happy place."

4

You rank *adventuresome* near the bottom of your personal attributes.

5

You don't want to be a fish on the other side of the pond.

6

You cannot imagine attending a college that doesn't participate in the Bowl Championship Series.

7

You consider ketchup to be a necessary food group.

8

You refuse to remove your shoes for airline security.

9

You suffer from xenophobia (a fear of foreigners).

10

Word association: someone says "foreign," you say "debt."

Around 150,000 students choose to earn college credit outside the United States each year. While most of these students study for a year or less, a few intrepid souls have earned their entire degrees abroad, encouraged by the Department of Education's willingness to allow students to use federal financial aid at foreign schools. Whether you decide to study nearby in Toronto or far away in Hong Kong, when it comes to choosing a college, your horizons just got a whole lot broader.

If you decide to explore studying abroad, you'll be happy to know you have a world of options. Foreign schools include both institutions fully accredited by U.S. accreditation bodies as well as non-American institutions that grant their own degrees. If you want to study in a foreign environment but still want to pursue an American-style education taught in English, you might want to choose one of the colleges fully accredited to grant degrees recognized by U.S. accreditation agencies.

You can also apply directly to a foreign school designed primarily for native students. These colleges teach in their local languages and grant degrees that don't necessarily have a U.S. equivalent. Being that some of the most prestigious colleges in the world are located outside the United States, it's no wonder that more and more students have decided to earn foreign degrees. Who knows? It might even be the right choice for you.

10 American Universities Abroad

Each of these schools is accredited by U.S. accrediting agencies:

1. The American University of Rome
2. The American University of Paris
3. The American University of Athens
4. The American University in Cairo
5. The American University in Bulgaria
6. The American University of Beirut
7. The American University of Puerto Rico
8. The American University of Sharjah (United Arab Emirates)
9. Richmond, The American International University in London
10. The American College of Thessaloniki

At a Glance

Deciding to attend a foreign school involves doing a *lot* of research. Whether it's establishing your ability to speak a foreign language, determining your financial aid options, or understanding the admissions requirements, you have a lot of homework ahead of you. But the rewards, which include living in an exciting new place and meeting people from all around the world, will no doubt be worth the extra preparation. The following 10 things you gotta know about foreign schools will help give you a better idea of what lies ahead.

1. Selectivity

The eight national universities of Japan admit only 15,000 students each year out of a total applicant pool of 1.5 million—which means only 1 percent of applicants gain admission.

If you thought Harvard was picky about its applicants, wait until you submit your application to one of the top-tier colleges overseas. Oxford and Cambridge in England, the Sorbonne in France, and the University of Tokyo all have much more difficult entry requirements than any American school.

Fortunately, you can find at least a few less selective foreign schools, many of which eagerly recruit American students and some of which even have quotas for the number of American students they enroll. You'll find these Americanized foreign schools slightly more selective than their counterparts within the United States, but you still have an excellent chance of gaining admission if you get good grades in high school. If you have the desire to attend a foreign school, the world really is your oyster.

2. Reputation

The American Universities in Bulgaria, Paris, Rome, and Athens admit over half of their applicants, and the American University in Puerto Rico offers admission to nearly every applicant.

Existing for seven hundred years gives a college plenty of time to work on its reputation—and no fewer than ten colleges are at least four hundred years older than Harvard. Even some relatively young schools have already established world-class programs that put them on par with the elite American universities:

- The University of Cambridge has produced eighty Nobel Prize winners
- Twenty-two Nobel winners have either studied or taught at the Swiss Federal Institute of Technology

Citizens of foreign nations hold most colleges in high esteem. Whereas college may seem like a natural next step in the United States, relatively few high school graduates go on to attend college in most of the rest of the world. You'll probably find that the members of the college community, from administrators to teachers to students, represent the best and the brightest of what their countries have to offer.

Despite schools' excellent reputations abroad, you should consider how American companies or grad schools will view your degree when (if) you return home. A degree from the University of Amsterdam may carry considerable weight in the Netherlands, but what passes for prestige abroad sometimes results in perplexity back home. Regardless of where you go, keep good records of your academic achievements, and, if possible, put together a portfolio of your accolades from your foreign college.

3. Cost

Attending a foreign college can be expensive. Most of the American Universities charge around $15,000 per year in tuition and fees, while Richmond, the American International University in London, charges around $32,000 for tuition, room, and board.

When thinking about costs, consider expenses not associated with attending an American school, such as these:

- Much higher airfare or transportation costs
- The costs of processing travel visas
- Health insurance and vaccination requirements
- The exchange-rate loss you may suffer by needing to pay tuition in euros or another foreign currency

10

Really Old Schools

1

University of Naples, Naples, Italy: 1,224 years old

2

University of Padua, Padua, Italy: 1,222 years old

3

Salamanca University, Salamanca, Spain: 1,218 years old

4

University of Cambridge, Cambridge, England: 1,209 years old

5

University of Modena, Modena, Italy: 1,175 years old

6

University of Paris, Paris, France: 1,150 years old

7

University of Oxford, Oxford, England: 1,096 years old

8

University of Bologna, Bologna, Italy: 1,088 years old

9

Al-Azhar University, Cairo, Egypt: 988 years old

10

Hunan University, Changsha, China: 976 years old

You should also remember that you probably won't be permitted to work in the foreign country where you study, which could mean no primary source of income.

Don't let the costs immediately scare you off—you have some options. The Department of Education has assigned over five hundred foreign colleges a school code that, in theory, authorizes them to process federal financial aid, almost always restricted to Stafford loans. The U.S. government also has several scholarship programs for both undergraduate and graduate students who wish to study overseas. The Institute of International Education (www. iie.org) has information about a host of scholarship programs.

Living and studying in London, Paris, or Tokyo can be very expensive, but picking a college in a smaller community or in a developing country can bring substantially lower costs. Many students in Eastern Europe, South Asia, and Africa pay $100 per month or less for room and board. Also, some international schools may not charge you much tuition. The American University of Puerto Rico charges less than $5,000 per year in tuition, while l'Ecole Polytechnique, one of France's most prestigious colleges, charges no fees whatsoever to international exchange students who qualify for admission.

4. Academics

You'll find that the American Universities abroad model their curriculum, teaching, credit structure, and degree programs on the education system in the United States. The courses will even be taught in English, meaning that lacking mastery of a foreign language shouldn't stop you from applying. Both class sizes and student bodies will probably be quite small, and these schools typically follow either the quarter or semester system, so you can still

10

U.S. COLLEGES
That Send 80 Percent of Their Students Abroad

1

Antioch College (Ohio)

2

Austin College (Texas)

3

Carleton College (Minnesota)

4

Centre College (Kentucky)

5

College of Saint Benedict (Minnesota)

6

DePauw University (Indiana)

7

Dickinson College (Pennsylvania)

8

Earlham College (Indiana)

9

Elon University (North Carolina)

10

Goshen College (Indiana)

look forward to winter, spring, and summer breaks to recover from all your studying.

Academics at non-American-based foreign universities might be a different story. For one thing, your studies might be much more intense than you'll find in most American colleges. Hoping to use your multiple-choice strategies to pass those final exams? Leave your number 2 pencils at home and bring a foreign language dictionary instead. Many colleges overseas have a long tradition of giving oral examinations during finals.

If this sounds a lot like graduate school, there's a reason. Many foreign colleges consider their first-year university programs to be equivalent to upperclass or even graduate studies at American schools. Some of these foreign schools may even require that American students already have an American bachelor's degree before applying for their baccalaureate programs.

5. Campus Life

Some students who study abroad are pleasantly surprised to find a vibrant campus life at their overseas schools. This is very important for American students, very few of whom will be allowed to take on part-time jobs or have the luxury of returning home frequently for visits. Fortunately, foreign schools often emphasize the importance of incorporating student activities into the academic curriculum, giving you plenty of things to do when not in class. The goal of the Student Life Department at the American College of Thessaloniki, for example, reads almost exactly like the goals of similar schools in the United States: *to foster intellectual, emotional, and physical growth and leadership potential in an environment that supports and challenges the student population.*

So don't worry about missing out on extracurricular activities. You can participate in athletic clubs, social events, and career counseling, among other things, just like you would back home. Getting involved will also help you improve those foreign language skills. As long as you don't expect helmets, shoulder pads, and cheerleaders, you can even show your school spirit by rooting for the football team.

10

HIGHLY PRESTIGIOUS
Foreign Schools

1

Oxford and Cambridge Universities
(www.cam.ac.uk and www.ox.ac.uk)

2

University of Tokyo (www.u-tokyo.ac.jp)

3

University of Paris Sorbonne (www.univ-paris1.fr)

4

University of Toronto (www.utoronto.ca)

5

University of Utrecht (www.uu.nl)

6

Technische Universität München (www.tu-muenchen.de)

7

Australian National University (www.anu.edu.au)

8

Moscow State University (www.msu.ru)

9

University of Copenhagen (www.ku.dk)

10

Swiss Federal Institute of Technology in Zurich (www.ethz.ch)

6. Residential Life

Choosing a foreign school means you probably won't have the option of living at home with Mom and Dad, and, because you'll be living in a new country, renting your own apartment may present too great an obstacle. Foreign schools often have dormitory-style residence halls available for students, and, as in the United States, you'll probably have a roommate or two. Many foreign colleges have trained student-affairs staff who can help make your residential life experience more rewarding.

Your room at a foreign school could be a studio flat in a historic part of ancient Rome, or it could be a triple-occupancy flat in Bulgaria with cold war–era furnishings.

An option students find especially popular in developing nations is to board with a local family. In addition to helping you learn the language and culture of the locals, living with a host family can save you a significant amount of money. You may want to see if your college will help you find a suitable host family, since going about this on your own could be difficult unless you are thoroughly familiar with the local language and customs.

7. Atmosphere

Students familiar with elite or liberal arts colleges in the United States might not find overseas schools to be the least bit foreign. After all, we based our higher education on foreign college systems, primarily in Western Europe. Many college towns in the United States even bear the names of cities boasting educational excellence abroad:

- Athens, Georgia (University of Georgia)
- Cambridge, Massachusetts (Harvard and MIT)
- Oxford, Ohio (Miami University)

Small class sizes, rigorous academic programs, and high standards typify the majority of foreign colleges selected by American students.

U.S. INSTITUTIONS
That Send the Most Students Abroad

1

New York University: 1,872 students

2

Michigan State University: 1,819 students

3

University of Texas at Austin: 1,591 students

4

University of Pennsylvania: 1,461 students

5

Georgetown University: 1,412 students

6

University of Wisconsin–Madison: 1,340 students

7

Boston University: 1,330 students

8

University of Arizona: 1,326 students

9

Penn State University: 1,270 students

10

University of Georgia: 1,268 students

Just about everyone who has spent significant time studying overseas will tell you that the experience changed their lives. Living outside your comfort zone, surrounded by people from all over the world, will give you a humbling and broader perspective. And if you really want to become fluent in a second or third language, you really have no choice but to study abroad.

The big things will certainly stand out in your head as you consider choosing a foreign college: reading Shakespeare along the banks of the river Avon, listening to "Claire de Lune" in the shadow of the Eiffel Tower, or studying the painted frescoes of the Sistine Chapel. But the everyday events, such as buying toothpaste using improvised hand gestures, will teach you just as much as what you learn in the classroom. The atmosphere of your foreign college experience will be as diverse as the world itself, introducing you to new cultures, cuisines, and class-mates.

If you really seek a change of pace, consider choosing a non-American college in a country outside of Europe. Studying in the Middle East, Asia, or Africa will introduce you not only to a new educational and language system but also to new customs, manners, and ways of thinking.

8. Students

Compared to the rest of the world, American students study abroad in miniscule numbers—perhaps unsurprising, given the enormous number of local college choices and our relative geographic isolation. The result is that students who choose to enroll in a foreign school are a select bunch. Some of their characteristics include:

- Curiousity
- Intrepidity
- Fascination with the outside world
- A sense of adventure
- Tendency to thrive on unfamiliar situations
- A good sense of our role in an international world
- A realization that they are ambassadors of the United States

If you hate change, taking risks, and meeting new people who may not speak your language or understand your fascination with songs from the eighties, choosing a foreign school may not be the best option for you.

The student bodies at the American Universities abroad are overwhelmingly international. Your non-American classmates, whether from the host nation or another country, will likely be extremely bright, as fewer students from other foreign countries typically go to college. Since those who do go represent the most academically gifted students from their respective countries, you might be intimidated at first. Just remember that surrounding yourself with talented individuals is one of the surest ways to become a better student yourself.

9. Professors

The good news about professors overseas is that the idea of using graduate students to teach college seems to be limited mostly to American institutions. Your teacher will undoubtedly be a highly qualified expert in his or her field. The professor will also likely have very high expectations of all his or her students, regardless of national origin, so be prepared for a challenging level of instruction.

You might not be used to the level of respect accorded to professors in other countries. If you're transferring from a liberal arts college in America where you're on a first-name basis with your teacher and are accustomed to openly disagreeing with his or her lessons, you may have to make some slight adjustments. Overseas, professors are the undisputed experts and leaders of the curriculum, and there may be a little less interaction and classroom equality than what you're used to. If you're accustomed to blurting out your ideas in the middle of the teacher's lecture, you might want to hold back until you learn the classroom pecking order.

You'll definitely need to brush up your communication skills by the time finals roll around. Foreign professors tend to rely much less on Scantron or other multiple-choice style tests than their U.S. counterparts.

10. The Intangibles

Small class sizes, rigorous academic programs, and high standards typify the majority of foreign colleges selected by American students. For the most part, these colleges are located in major urban centers, including some of the greatest cities in civilization. Rome, Paris, and London, in particular, attract large numbers of U.S. students. But major, prestigious universities can also be found in just about every great city, including Tokyo, Cairo, Vienna, and Moscow, to name just a few.

In addition to differences in language and culture, you'll face legal and financial hurdles—simply navigating the passport and visa requirements can become an education in itself. You'll also face concerns about whether your credits will transfer back to an American college, homesickness, and staying healthy.

Depending on which country you choose for your new home, you may also need to keep up to date with travel and safety warnings. In fact, one of the first things you should do is register with the nearest U.S. embassy or consulate. Don't let this caution keep you from considering a foreign school—by and large, studying abroad is no more dangerous than studying in the United States.

Is This the Right Choice?

Adding international experience and a foreign language or two to your résumé will make you more competitive when you start looking for a career or grad school. But with the romance and adventure comes extra work. If you're self-sufficient, eager for new challenges, and unafraid of working hard in an unfamiliar environment, a foreign school might be the perfect choice for your college education.

However, even if you're not yet sure whether a foreign school is right for you, you still have study-abroad options if you choose an American college. Many U.S. colleges have outstanding study-abroad programs and send large numbers of students overseas for a year or less.

Whether you decide to study for four years or a semester at an American-based foreign school or a prestigious overseas university, you can hardly go wrong by choosing to add a little international education to your plate. Most students who study abroad will tell you it was the best choice they ever made.

10
TREASURE SCHOOLS

"He had been a lad of whom something was expected. . . . That he would be successful in an original way, or go to the dogs in an original way, seemed equally probable."

Thomas Hardy
The Return of the Native

10

CLUES

They Might *Not* Be for You

1

You require traditional, tried-and-true teaching.

2

You're hoping to breeze through at least a couple of easy lectures.

3

The thought of designing your own major sends you
to your "happy place."

4

You rank *conformity* near the top of your personal attributes.

5

You don't want to think outside the pond.

6

You cannot imagine attending a college that doesn't offer
letter or number grades.

7

You consider teaching assistants to be a necessary evil.

8

You refuse to attend a college that your grandparents
have never heard of.

9

You suffer from cenophobia (a fear of new things or ideas).

10

Word association: someone says "treasure," you say "buried."

Some colleges just seem to defy convention. They've carved out a unique niche within the field of higher education by producing outstanding graduates, using methods that break the mold. While other schools continue to teach the same way year after year, these colleges take a different approach. They are the hidden treasures of the American college system.

These treasure colleges believe that remaining devoted to student development doesn't mean staying committed to the status quo. Other schools may focus on letter grades, required core classes outside of your major, and measuring your degree progress by how many hoops you can jump through. But the treasure colleges understand that not every student learns the same way. Instead, they concentrate on developing a curriculum that meets *your* needs.

More important, they believe the college years should do more than simply teach a skill. Students who graduate from treasure colleges leave with an understanding of leadership, a commitment to making the world a better place, and a passion for lifelong learning. If you've ever sat in a traditional classroom and thought, "This just isn't for me," a treasure college might be what you've been waiting for.

At a Glance

After looking far and wide for the college that's right for you, you might feel like the perfect school simply doesn't exist. Maybe you're a true original, or maybe your criteria are so unique that a meaningful search presents too great a challenge. Treasure colleges don't necessarily fit neatly into any one category. They can be either public or private, coed or gender specific, large or small, urban or rural. Only a few schools have the intangible qualities needed for a

In describing the characteristics of these schools, some scholars use the term *Paideia*—an education whose goal is to form an enlightened and active mind.

COLLEGES

That Make the Grade Matter

The following colleges offer alternative grading policies by offering narrative evaluations instead of or in addition to traditional letter grades.

1

Purchase College (New York)

2

University of California, Santa Cruz

3

Reed College (Oregon)

4

New College of Florida

5

Hampshire College (Massachusetts)

6

Bennington College (Vermont)

7

Alverno College (Wisconsin)

8

The Evergreen State College (Washington)

9

Prescott College (Arizona)

10

Sarah Lawrence College (New York)

truly life-changing education. What they have in common is an ability to move students to accomplish greatness. So with you in mind, here are 10 things you gotta know about what makes these schools so different.

1. Selectivity

Even though the treasure colleges provide an extraordinary education, they often do so just under the radar. This means that many of these schools have reasonable selectivity rates, with several admitting the majority of applicants.

Not every one of these schools is a well-kept secret. Trinity College in Hartford, Connecticut, has offered such an outstanding curriculum since 1823 that today it must turn away almost 70 percent of applicants. But by and large, if you have your eyes on a treasure college, the odds of you finding one that will grant you admission is much better than you probably think.

2. Reputation

Many treasure schools have superb international reputations, even though they may not do things according to the mainstream. They're held in especially high esteem by the nation's top graduate and professional schools, as a high proportion of graduates continue their education after earning their bachelor's degrees. In particular, treasure school graduates benefit from an education that encourages them to be active learners, which often translates into outstanding public speaking and critical thinking skills, both of which serve them well in job and graduate school interviews.

Students at these colleges also benefit from quality instruction. Many treasure colleges hire the best faculty in the nation, who want to teach at colleges that emphasize undergraduate education. Having superb instructors

Prescott College, a hidden gem in Arizona, admits over 80 percent of its applicants.

Knox College in Illinois consistently ranks in the top 2 percent of colleges nationally in terms of producing successful Ph.D. candidates.

further adds to the reputation of these schools, a few of which have seen their applicant numbers skyrocket in recent years. Some alumni watch in amazement as the value of their degrees seems to appreciate each year as the esteem of their alma maters grow.

3. Cost

You know the saying, "The best things in life are sometimes free"? You'll be happy to know that it most definitely applies to higher education: some of the treasure colleges out there charge no tuition at all. For example, the College of the Ozarks in Missouri and Berea College in Kentucky offer world-class teaching and, in exchange for a little work, waive tuition for admitted students.

You can still find great bargains among the treasure colleges that do get around to charging tuition. State residents of California, for example, have access to some of the nation's true public college gems, including Humboldt State University, which charges residents less than $3,000 per year. Even among the more expensive private schools, several offer considerable financial aid award packages to students with need, meaning when it comes to treasure colleges, sharing the wealth is the name of the game.

4. Academics

Just because the treasure colleges do things differently doesn't mean they don't do things well. This is especially true when it comes to teaching. Unlike the major research universities, treasure colleges don't pawn off undergraduate students to teaching assistants. The faculty members at these schools don't believe in sacrificing an individual's freshman and sophomore years for the sake of adding to a college's list of publications or research grants. From the very first day, students at the treasure colleges are actively engaged in the learning process, developing critical thinking skills they'll carry with them throughout their education and careers.

Academics are marked at these schools by participation. Instead of a teacher delivering a lecture while students take notes, most classes are taught in the seminar style, and students are expected to share their ideas aloud. While this can seem intimidating, you should also realize that these colleges tend to be much less competitive than their peers. The New College in Florida offers a great model. Instead of assigning letter grades along the lines of a bell curve, professors take the time to write individual evaluations describing how you performed.

Students who transfer from traditional colleges often say that this approach to education improves their learning. Instead of concentrating on memorizing facts to get the top grade in class, students can focus on understanding the deeper meaning of their studies. Instead of trying to out-perform the other students in class, they feel free to cooperate with their classmates, making these schools true learning communities.

5. Campus Life

The sense of purpose and cooperation in these colleges' classrooms spills into the community. Treasure college campuses have built a strong reputation for concerned students, who often lead the nation in volunteerism and community service and in actively supporting the causes in which they believe. The true treasure schools foster a high level of campus participation instead of reining it in, since it represents a key component to an overall education.

Campus life at some treasure schools, however, might seem a little quiet, since many students understand the importance of learning firsthand about the rest of the world. Over 70 percent of Kentucky's Centre College students study abroad, and at Goshen College in Indiana, the students' travels are matched by the faculty, over half of whom have lived or worked abroad.

If you're interested in sports, special events, and concerts, not to worry. The treasure colleges offer these as well. Just don't be surprised if they're not their first priority.

Academics aren't the only things the treasure colleges do differently. Several unique mascots can be found at these schools, including the Presbyterian College Bluehose (a Scotsman clad in a kilt and wearing blue stockings). Presbyterian College is home to the world's largest bronze statue of a Scotsman.

Students at the tiny College of the Atlantic, in Maine, recently banded together to convince school leaders to stop doing business with companies linked to human rights abuses.

6. Residential Life

Because these treasure schools emphasize the importance of learning both inside and outside of the classroom, most have extremely high percentages of students living on campus. Presbyterian College in South Carolina houses over 90 percent of all enrolled students, and several smaller schools actually have 100 percent of students living on campus.

Dormitories at these schools are far more than merely a place to hang your hat. Treasure colleges have developed innovative residence life programs that offer study assistance, community activities, and even counseling services to their students. Before you choose to live off campus, don't overlook the main reason many students choose to enroll at a treasure school: to become part of a true community of scholars and activists. The friendships that last a lifetime aren't such a bad benefit, either.

7. Atmosphere

The atmosphere of a treasure college can be summed up in one word: *involvement.*

Students and teachers don't choose treasure schools to blend quietly into the background. If you were hoping for a large lecture hall where you could disappear among three hundred faces in the crowd, you might want to reconsider. If you think you have nothing you could possibly contribute to a discussion, either in class or among new friends gathering at the student union, then a treasure school might overwhelm you.

On the other hand, one of these schools might help you prove yourself wrong. A treasure school depends on its community members, and these people have an uncanny ability to draw out the student you never knew you could be. This is particularly true at the schools that focus less on grades and more on student outcomes.

When it comes to diversity, one of the first things you'll learn is that individual differences include many factors you might not have considered. These schools, even those that are gender specific, can be extremely diverse in the sense that their students come from various backgrounds in income, origin, and beliefs. Bringing individuals with different ideas together for the common cause of making the world a better place is the hallmark of the treasure schools.

8. Students

The treasure colleges might be the only schools where students are 100 percent determined and 0 percent cutthroat. Do you remember that kid in high school who never seemed to care about her grades, but still seemed as intelligent as the school valedictorian? Those who choose a treasure college are much less interested in a school's reputation and much more concerned about a school's commitment to its students.

Treasure college students always seem to remember that they're the most important assets of any school. Whereas a student who gains admission to an ultraselective elite college is usually too elated to complain about being treated like a number, treasure college students expect better. They never forget that the reason a college exists is to serve its students, and not the other way around.

Treasure colleges graduates continue to be enamored with their colleges long after they graduate. Centre College alumni rank first in the nation for the percentage of students making gifts.

9. Professors

Treasure college professors might be better described as coaches or facilitators. They certainly have plenty of wisdom to impart—but when a teacher believes that every student has an equal contribution to make, the richness of classroom learning attains even greater heights.

PUBLIC
Treasure Schools

1

Colorado School of Mines

2

College of Charleston (South Carolina)

3

Humboldt State University (California)

4

University of California, Santa Cruz

5

New College of Florida

6

Fairhaven College at Western Washington University

7

University of Montevallo (Alabama)

8

Miami University (Ohio)

9

The Evergreen State College (Washington)

10

Binghamton University (New York)

Treasure school professors seem to have a great deal of faith in the abilities of their students, and if you visit a treasure college campus, you'll probably hear a great deal about joint faculty/student research. Independent study or research projects are also extremely popular at these schools, allowing students to create entirely new programs that combine the different topics they want to study. Many treasure school faculty members, like the teachers at Austin College in Texas, even encourage students to combine independent study with study abroad. Anyone who has ever been encouraged to exceed his or her abilities will truly feel at home at a treasure school.

10. The Intangibles

A common story told by treasure college graduates revolves around the initial difficulty they had in convincing their parents to support their choice. These are definitely not the traditional schools your parents or grandparents may have had in mind when they started your college savings account. The first thing you may need to consider if you feel a treasure college is right for you is how you're going to break the news to a skeptical relative. The decision is ultimately yours—but it won't hurt to have some solid, well-thought-out reasons for why this particular school is the perfect one for you.

Because college is an investment, the first factor you should investigate is the college's results. When you visit a campus with your parents, make sure you ask plenty of questions about graduate school and job placement rates. Ask the admissions counselor to provide a sampling of successful or famous alumni. And talk with current students about how they feel the school has made a difference in their lives. Choosing a treasure college may take a little extra investigation, but nothing worthwhile comes easy.

Although many treasure colleges are labeled "alternative," they are often imitated by the mainstream. In the late 1970s, Hampshire College became the first school in America to divest from companies in South Africa as a protest of apartheid. A host of institutions soon followed suit.

10 Treasure Schools

Wondering how to find a treasure school? The following descriptions should help get you started. The following 10 schools have several characteristics in common:

- A demonstrated commitment to students both inside and outside of the classroom
- A focus on the individual
- A dedication to serving others in society
- The creation of a community of learners

Even if none of the following colleges fit your needs, they should give you some food for thought about what a treasure school has to offer—and whether one might be right for you.

1. Berea College (Kentucky)

At Berea College, the best things in life are free. Students at this truly unique liberal arts school receive full-tuition scholarships in exchange for ten to fifteen hours per week of work. But they also receive a superior education from a faculty that is consistently regarded as among the best and most committed in the nation. Combine this with a philosophy dedicated to serving the community and the result is graduates with both the tools and drive to change the world. See **www.berea.edu** for more information.

2. Reed College (Oregon)

Perhaps no school in the country challenges its students more intensely than Reed College in Portland, Oregon. Despite a deemphasis on grades, Reed students consistently achieve academic excellence and recognition. Reed has produced 56 Fulbright fellows, 104 National Science Foundation fellows, 2 Pulitzer Prize winners, 31 Rhodes Scholars, and 2 MacArthur Genius Award winners. If you have what it takes to meet the academic demands, Reed could be the perfect school for you. See **www.reed.edu** for more information.

3. St. John's College (New Mexico/Maryland)

St. John's College, with campuses in Santa Fe and Annapolis, is a coed liberal arts college that offers one of the most distinctive degree programs in the nation. Students at St. John's don't use textbooks, and they are not subjected to lectures. Instead, they read from the "great books" and discuss the meanings of those texts with their classmates and instructors. The emphasis is not on memorizing knowledge but on *understanding* knowledge. Like Reed College, St. John's students go on to graduate school and win prestigious awards at rates as high as any Ivy League school. Check out **www.sjcsf.edu** to learn more.

In 1858, Cornell College in Iowa became the first institution of higher education west of the Mississippi to grant women the same rights and privileges as men. In 1858, Mary Fellows became the first woman in Iowa to earn a bachelor's degree.

4. The Evergreen State College (Washington)

Private colleges haven't cornered the market on truly unique teaching and learning: the Evergreen State College offers a liberal arts education at public-school tuition rates. Students at Evergreen select interdisciplinary programs that combine several subject areas and receive narrative evaluations of their performance instead of grades. The students also provide feedback for their instructors at the end of each quarter. Evergreen students carry this same level of interactivity into the community and are among the most socially active and responsible students in the country. Take a look at **www.evergreen.edu** for more information.

5. Deep Springs College (Nevada)

The only all-male college and the only two-year college in this list, Deep Springs might very well be the most unconventional school in the country. With an average class size of four, perhaps no other college can match the depth of discussion students have with their teachers and class-

Treasured Alumni

1

Matt Groening, creator of *The Simpsons* (The Evergreen State College)

2

Robery Noyce, founder of Intel (Grinnell College)

3

Robert Mills, architect of the Washington Monument
(College of Charleston)

4

Lorine Niedecker, only woman Objectivist poet (Beloit College)

5

Frances McDormand and William H. Macy, co-stars, *Fargo*
(Bethany College)

6

James Garfield, twentieth president of the United States (Hiram College)

7

Isaac Tigrett, founder of the Hard Rock Café and House of Blues
(Centre College)

8

Hiram Rhoades Revels, first African American senator (Knox College)

9

Edward Albee, playwright (Trinity College)

10

Parker Posey, actor (Purchase College)

mates. Located on a remote ranch in the Nevada desert, students must also work in exchange for the free tuition. Students pay only for travel, books, and incidental costs. What they get in return is an intense two-year education. Read more at **www.deepsprings.edu**.

6. University of California, Santa Cruz

UC Santa Cruz, the only other public college on this list, employed narrative evaluations instead of letter grades until recently, when the number of enrolled students surpassed 15,000. Nevertheless, UC Santa Cruz is still able to offer the best of an intimate education with a big-campus feel. UC Santa Cruz students go on to Ph.D. programs at a rate that rivals any of the elite colleges. See **www.ucsc.edu** for more information.

7. Grinnell College (Iowa)

With the highest rate of Peace Corps volunteers of any college in the nation, tiny Grinnell College in Iowa lives up to a reputation of service before self. This sense of helping others begins in the classroom, and with a 10 to 1 student to faculty ratio, Grinnell ensures that each student participates in an active learning experience that is the signature of a quality liberal arts education. Check out Grinnell's website, **www.grinnell.edu**.

8. Mount Holyoke (Massachusetts)

The only women's college on the list, this South Hadley, Massachusetts, school is actually the first women's college in the country and the longest continuously running women's college in the world. This academically rigorous yet intimate campus has a reputation for producing great writers. See **www.mtholyoke.edu** for more information.

9. Earlham College (Indiana)

Students at Earlham College know they're different from the beginning. Whereas most students across the country go to college to get a better job, Earlham students are far more interested in becoming better people. This tiny, Indiana liberal arts college, where students are on a first-name basis with faculty, produces graduates with a commitment to helping others but who also go on to great things. Check out **www.earlham.edu**.

10. Albertson College (Idaho)

Who would think that a tiny college in Idaho would consistently rank as one of the best liberal arts college deals year after year? Combine a rigorous academic course load with faculty members who really care about student development and the result is an impressive list of graduates that includes Pulitzer Prize winners, Academy Award winners, and two former governors. See **www.albertson.edu** for more information.

Is This the Right Choice?

More often than not, treasure colleges provide a liberal arts curriculum. They offer small class sizes taught by caring professors, encourage active student participation both inside and outside of the classroom, and teach critical thinking skills instead of rote memorization. Because they offer unique programs and teaching methods, they attract a lot of students who you wouldn't necessarily describe as "mainstream." Many of the colleges listed in this chapter attract a relatively high percentage of older students who found out about these unique institutions only after they enrolled elsewhere.

But that doesn't mean these schools should be stereotyped as "alternative" schools. In fact, one of the striking characteristics of the treasure colleges is the high quality of research and development that often goes on there. And since these colleges create a participatory learning environment, much of that research and development is led by the students themselves, many of whom may have underperformed in more traditional educational settings.

As you try to find the college that's right for you, consider the colleges that complement you and your personality. There's a school out there that's as unique as you are—and a treasure school just may be the one.

EPILOGUE

"[N]ow we come to the passage. You can just see a little peep of the passage in Looking-glass House, if you leave the door of our drawing-room wide open; and it's very likely our passage as far as you can see, only you know it may be quite different on beyond."

Lewis Carroll
Through the Looking Glass

You can be forgiven if you've run out of breath—all these choices can be overwhelming. But having choices is a good thing—you just need to use your knowledge wisely.

To make your decision, you should first try to narrow your choices to one of the 10 basic types of colleges. If you're a budding artist with a desire to share your work with the world, you might be a great candidate for a fine arts school. If you need a practical skill but want to reserve the option of eventually earning a bachelor's degree, a community college could be just the thing. If you've been accepted into Harvard—well, you might want to stick with Harvard.

Your next steps won't be so hard. There are basically 10 things you should do to determine which college you'll call home for the next few years:

1. Find the Schools

Word of mouth, online resources, and books will provide you with good leads about what schools are out there. Be wary of any college guides older than three or four years: many colleges, particularly private, for-profit schools, have gone out of business in the past few years, though they may still be listed in printed publications.

2. Gather Information

Visit **www.sparkcollege.com** for basic information on schools, including:

- Admissions factors
- Faculty/student ratio
- Graduation rates
- Types of majors offered
- Acceptance rate
- Application deadlines
- Cost

3. Talk to a Counselor

You shouldn't contact school administrators wildly, since you'll likely be swamped with promotional emails and mailings. Consider this level of communication as a more focused level of research—and be aware that admissions counselors will likely give you canned information that presents the college in the best possible light. Don't lose sight of your real concerns, which may include:

- Whether the faculty/student ratio applies to each individual class or represents an average across the entire school
- How likely it is that you'll be able to enroll in your first-choice classes as a first-year student
- How many students graduate within four years

Don't be afraid to take charge of the conversation and ask serious questions.

4. Compare Your Options

After you've collected the hard facts and spoken to college representatives, you should narrow your options down to schools worthy of a visit. Don't be afraid if your choices don't all look alike. Your goal here is not to pick the final school but a good cross-section of potential.

Be prepared to contact the admissions counselors at the schools you pick for visits. A good question to ask is, "Are there any other schools that offer a similar college experience as yours?" Admissions counselors definitely know who makes up their competition, and, surprisingly, they'll often share this information with prospective students.

5. Visit Schools

The college visitation process could be your most daunting—and expensive—task. You'll need to make some strategic choices. If you search locally, you could visit ten colleges or more. If your search includes several distant campuses, however, you may not be able to visit as many schools, due to both time and cost constraints.

No matter how many schools you visit, take the visits seriously. The admissions counselors will probably take you on a predesigned tour that highlights the best a campus has to offer—but you should also explore on your own. Try to sit in on a class, and talk to students afterward about whether they feel they made the right choice.

One piece of advice regarding the costs involved with visits: you may not know this, but when you apply for federal financial aid, the Department of Education weights your own income and assets more heavily toward the amount they calculate you can pay for college. If you've received cash gifts recently, you might want to use that money to pay for visiting colleges, rather than having your parents foot the bill. You'll likely save yourself financial aid you otherwise would have lost.

6. Apply

If college applications were free, you could theoretically apply to dozens, if not hundreds, of schools. But some of these fees can be fairly high. The MIT application fee, for example, will set you back a cool $65. You need to choose wisely.

You should read each application closely, making sure you understand the application requirements. Many applications may seem straightforward, but the process at selective schools can be intimidating, involving essays and interviews. You may also have to decide whether you want to apply early through "Early Decision" or "Early Action." Early Decision applications are binding decisions intended for students who have definitely chosen one college. Early Action applications allow students to consider other colleges.

7. Learn About Financial Aid

You'll need to complete the appropriate financial aid applications as soon as possible after January 1 of the year in which you'll begin college. The colleges that accept you for admission should then process your financial aid award.

In a perfect world, financial aid wouldn't matter at all. You'd simply choose the college that offered the programs you want in the environment you're looking for. But since you don't want to graduate with debt you'll be hard-pressed to manage, you need to seriously consider financial aid. Compare the award letters you receive, looking at which schools will offer you the education you seek while leaving you with as little debt as possible.

8. Decide

With any luck, you can make your final decision based on no more than two or three schools, each of which seems perfect in its own way, and none of which will break the bank. So what's the final thing you've gotta know about making this ultimate choice?

It's up to you now. Once you get to this last step, you need to trust your instincts and pick the college that feels right. Don't worry if you have a little lingering doubt about your choice, as many major life decisions you'll make will leave you feeling similarly light-headed. Rest assured that in the end, you can be successful at any college lucky enough to land you.

9. Keep Working

You've done your homework. You've made your choice. It's time to celebrate.

Well, not just yet. You probably have a few weeks, or even months, before high school graduation—and you should know that schools can rescind their offers of admission to students who slack off in their academics. You need to keep your grades up. Not only will this keep you in good graces with your new school, but it will set a good pattern for the upcoming year, when you'll learn what hard work *really* is.

10. Plan Your Move

Your first week at college is *not* the time to worry about deposits, a new driver's license, textbooks, dorm room furniture, and the million other details that come with settling in to a new place. You should prepare as much as possible during the summer so that you can focus on the things that really matter once you arrive on campus.

APPENDIX

State Higher Ed Agencies

Alabama Commission on Higher Education
PO Box 302000
Montgomery, AL 36130-2000
Phone: 800-960-7773
Fax: 334-242-0268
Website: http://www.ache.state.al.us

Alaska Commission on Postsecondary Education
3030 Vintage Boulevard
Juneau, AK 99801-7100
Phone: 800-441-2962
Fax: 907-465-5316
Website: http://www.state.ak.us/acpe

Arizona Commission for Postsecondary Education
2020 North Central Avenue, Suite 550
Phoenix, AZ 85004-4503
Phone: 602-258-2435
Fax: 602-258-2483
Website: http://www.azhighered.org

Arkansas Department of Higher Education
114 East Capitol
Little Rock, AR 72201-3818
Phone: 501-371-2000
Fax: 501-371-2001
Website: http://www.arkansashighered.com

California Student Aid Commission
PO Box 419027
Rancho Cordova, CA 95741-9027
Phone: 888-224-7268
Fax: 916-526-8004
Website: http://www.csac.ca.gov

Colorado Commission on Higher Education
1380 Lawrence Street, Suite 1200
Denver, CO 80204
Phone: 303-866-2723
Fax: 303-866-4266
Website: http://www.state.co.us/cche

Connecticut Department of Higher Education
61 Woodland Street
Hartford, CT 06105-2326
Phone: 800-842-0229
Fax: 860-947-1310
Website: http://www.ctdhe.org

Delaware Higher Education Commission
Carvel State Office Building, Fifth Floor
820 North French Street
Wilmington, DE 19801
Phone: 800-292-7935
Fax: 302-577-6765
Website: http://www.doe.state.de.us/high-ed

District of Columbia State Education Office
441 Fourth Street, NW
Suite 350 North
Washington, DC 20001
Phone: 877-485-6751
Fax: 202-727-2834
Website: http://seo.dc.gov

Florida Department of Education
Office of the Commissioner
Turlington Building, Suite 1514
325 West Gaines Street
Tallahassee, FL 32399
Phone: 850-245-0505
Fax: 850-245-9667
Website: http://www.fldoe.org

Georgia Student Finance Commission
State Loans Division
2082 East Exchange Place, Suite 230
Tucker, GA 30084
Phone: 800-505-4732
Fax: 770-724-9263
Website: http://www.gsfc.org

Hawaii State Postsecondary Education
Commission
2444 Dole Street, Room 209
Honolulu, HI 96822-2302
Phone: 808-956-8213
Fax: 808-956-5156
Website: http://www.hern.hawaii.edu/
hern

Idaho State Board of Education
P.O. Box 83720
Boise, ID 83720-0037
Phone: 208-334-2270
Fax: 208-334-2632
Website: http://www.idahoboardofed.org

Illinois Student Assistance
Commission
1755 Lake Cook Road
Deerfield, IL 60015-5209
Phone: 800-899-4722
Fax: 847-831-8549
Website: http://www.collegezone.com

State Student Assistance Commission
of Indiana
150 West Market Street, Suite 500
Indianapolis, IN 46204-2811
Phone: 317-232-2350
Fax: 317-232-3260
Website: http://www.ssaci.in.gov

Iowa College Student Aid Commission
200 10th Street, Fourth Floor
Des Moines, IA 50309
Phone: 800-383-4222
Fax: 515-242-3388
Website: http://www.iowacollegeaid.org

Kansas Board of Regents
Curtis State Office Building
1000 SW Jackson Street, Suite 520
Topeka, KS 66612-1368
Phone: 785-296-3421
Fax: 785-296-0983
Website: http://www.kansasregents.org

Kentucky Higher Education Assistance
Authority
P.O. Box 798
Frankfort, KY 40602-0798
Phone: 800-928-8926
Fax: 502-696-7496
Website: http://www.kheaa.com

Louisiana Office of Student Financial
Assistance
P.O. Box 91202
Baton Rouge, LA 70821-9202
Phone: 800-259-5626
Fax: 225-922-0790
Website: http://www.osfa.state.la.us

Finance Authority of Maine
P.O. Box 949
Augusta, ME 04332-0949
Phone: 800-228-3734
Fax: 207-623-0095
Website: http://www.famemaine.com

Maryland Higher Education Commission
839 Bestgate Road, Suite 400
Annapolis, MD 21401-3013
Phone: 410-260-4500
Fax: 410-974-5994
Website: http://www.mhec.state.md.us

Massachusetts Board of Higher Education
One Ashburton Place, Room 1401
Boston, MA 02108
Phone: 617-994-6950
Fax: 617-727-6397
Website: http://www.mass.edu

Massachusetts Higher Education Information Center
Boston Public Library
700 Boylston Street
Boston, MA 02116
Phone: 617-536-0200
Fax: 617-536-4737
Website: http://www.edinfo.org

Michigan Higher Education Assistance Authority
Office of Scholarships and Grants
P.O. Box 30462
Lansing, MI 48909-7962
Phone: 888-447-2687
Fax: 517-335-5984
Website: http://www.michigan.gov/mistudentaid

Minnesota Higher Education Services Office
1450 Energy Park Drive, Suite 350
Saint Paul, MN 55108-5227
Phone: 800-657-3866
Fax: 651-642-0675
Website: http://www.mheso.state.mn.us

Mississippi Office of Student Financial Aid
3825 Ridgewood Road
Jackson, MS 39211-6453
Phone: 601-432-6997
Fax: 601-432-6527
Website:
http://www.mississippiuniversities.com

Missouri Department of Higher Education
3515 Amazonas Drive
Jefferson City, MO 65109-5717
Phone: 800-473-6757
Fax: 573-751-6635
Website: http://www.dhe.mo.gov

Montana University System
2500 Broadway
P.O. Box 203101
Helena, MT 59620-3101
Phone: 406-444-6570
Fax: 406-444-1469
Website: http://www.montana.edu/wwwoche

Nebraska Coordinating Commission for Postsecondary Education
140 North Eighth Street, Suite 300
P.O. Box 95005
Lincoln, NE 68509-5005
Phone: 402-471-2847
Fax: 402-471-2886
Website: http://www.ccpe.state.ne.us/PublicDoc/CCPE/Default.asp

Nevada System of Higher Education
5550 W. Flamingo Rd., Suite C-1
Las Vegas, NV 89103
Phone: 702-889-8426
Fax: 702-889-8492
Website: http://system.nevada.edu

New Hampshire Postsecondary Education Commission
3 Barrell Court, Suite 300
Concord, NH 03301-8543
Phone: 603-271-2555
Fax: 603-271-2696
Website: http://www.state.nh.us/postsecondary

Commission on Higher Education (New Jersey)
20 West State Street
P.O. Box 542
Trenton, NJ 08625-0542
Phone: 609-292-4310
Fax: 609-292-7225
Website: http://www.state.nj.us/highereducation/index.htm

Higher Education Student Assistance Authority (New Jersey)
P.O. Box 540
Building 4
Quakerbridge Plaza
Trenton, NJ 08625-0540
Phone: 800-792-8670
Fax: 609-588-7389
Website: http://www.hesaa.org

New Mexico Commission on Higher Education
1068 Cerrillos Road
Santa Fe, NM 87505
Phone: 800-279-9777
Fax: 505-476-6511
Website: http://www.nmche.org

New York State Higher Education Services Corporation
99 Washington Avenue
Albany, NY 12255
Phone: 888-697-4372
Fax: 518-474-2839
Email: webmail@hesc.org
Website: http://www.hesc.org

North Carolina State Education Assistance Authority
P.O. Box 13663
Research Triangle Park, NC 27709-3663
Phone: 919-549-8614
Fax: 919-549-8481
Website: http://www.cfnc.org

North Dakota University System
North Dakota Student Financial Assistance Program
Department 215
600 East Boulevard Avenue
Bismarck, ND 58505-0230
Phone: 701-328-4114
Fax: 701-328-2961
Website: http://www.ndus.edu

Ohio Board of Regents
State Grants and Scholarships Department
57 East Main Street, Fourth Floor
Columbus, OH 43215
Phone: 888-833-1133
Fax: 614-752-5903
Website: http://www.regents.state.oh.us/sgs

Oklahoma State Regents for Higher Education
655 Research Parkway, Suite 200
Oklahoma City, OK 73104
Phone: 800-858-1840
Fax: 405-225-9230
Website: http://www.okhighered.org

Oregon Student Assistance Commission
1500 Valley River Drive, Suite 100
Eugene, OR 97401
Phone: 800-452-8807
Fax: 541-687-7419
Website: http://www.osac.state.or.us

Oregon University System
P.O. Box 3175
Eugene, OR 97403-0175
Phone: 541-346-5700
Fax: 541-346-5764
Website: http://www.ous.edu

Office of Postsecondary and Higher Education (Pennsylvania)
Department of Education
333 Market Street
Harrisburg, PA 17126
Phone: 717-787-5041
Fax: 717-772-3622
Website: http://www.pdehighered.state.
pa.us/higher/site/default.asp

Rhode Island Higher Education Assistance Authority
560 Jefferson Boulevard
Warwick, RI 02886
Phone: 800-922-9855
Fax: 401-732-3541
Website: http://www.riheaa.org

Rhode Island Office of Higher Education
301 Promenade Street
Providence, RI 02908-5748
Phone: 401-222-6560
Fax: 401-222-6111
Website: http://www.ribghe.org

South Carolina Commission on Higher Education
1333 Main Street, Suite 200
Columbia, SC 29201
Phone: 877-349-7183
Fax: 803-737-2297
Website: http://www.che400.state.sc.us

South Dakota Board of Regents
306 East Capitol Avenue, Suite 200
Pierre, SD 57501
Phone: 605-773-3455
Fax: 605-773-5320
Website: http://www.ris.sdbor.edu

Tennessee Higher Education Commission
Parkway Towers
404 James Robertson Parkway, Suite 1900
Nashville, TN 37243-0830
Phone: 615-741-3605
Fax: 615-741-6230
Website: http://www.state.tn.us/thec

Texas Higher Education Coordinating Board
P.O. Box 12788
Austin, TX 78711
Phone: 800-242-3062
Fax: 512-427-6127
Website: http://www.thecb.state.tx.us

Utah State Board of Regents
Gateway Center
60 South 400 West
Salt Lake City, UT 84101-1284
Phone: 801-321-7103
Fax: 801-321-7199
Website: http://www.utahsbr.edu

Vermont Student Assistance Corporation
Champlain Mill
1 Main Street, Third Floor
P.O. Box 2000
Winooski, VT 05404-2601
Phone: 800-642-3177
Fax: 802-654-3765
Website: http://www.vsac.org

State Council of Higher Education for Virginia
James Monroe Building
101 North 14th Street, Ninth Floor
Richmond, VA 23219
Phone: 804-225-2600
Fax: 804-225-2604
Website: http://www.schev.edu

Washington State Higher Education Coordinating Board
P.O. Box 43430
917 Lakeridge Way
Olympia, WA 98504-3430
Phone: 360-753-7800
Fax: 360-753-7808
Website: http://www.hecb.wa.gov

West Virginia Higher Education Policy Commission
1018 Kanawha Boulevard, East
Charleston, WV 25301
Phone: 304-558-2101
Fax: 304-558-5719
Website: http://www.hepc.wvnet.edu

Wisconsin Higher Educational Aids Board
131 West Wilson Street, Suite 902
Madison, WI 53703
Phone: 608-267-2206
Fax: 608-267-2808
Website: http://heab.state.wi.us

Wyoming Community College Commission
2020 Carey Avenue, Eighth Floor
Cheyenne, WY 82002
Phone: 307-777-7763
Fax: 307-777-6567
Website: http://commission.wcc.edu

ACKNOWLEDGMENTS

This guide is dedicated to Dr. Paul Fidler. I would like to think of it as simply one more way that Paul has been able to touch the lives of students. For over thirty-five years, he served as mentor, teacher, and friend to countless members of the University of South Carolina community, including the author. He is missed.

Special thanks also go out to Andrew Littell for his initial guidance on this project and, once again, to Margo Orlando for her editorial alchemy.

ABOUT THE AUTHOR

Brandon Rogers has held numerous student affairs positions over the past ten years, including at the University of South Carolina, Fort Hays State University in Kansas, and the Evergreen State College, where he served as an admissions counselor. He currently conducts research and writing for the Office of College Relations at Clover Park Technical College in Lakewood, Washington. He has attended several schools, including the University of Missouri, Lucian Blaga University in Romania, and the University of South Carolina, where he earned his master's degree in higher education. He is also the author of the book *10 Things You Gotta Know About Paying for College* (Spark Publishing, 2005).